HOME OFFICE RESEARCH STUDIES

32

Residential Treatment and its Effects on Delinquency

By D B Cornish and R V G Clarke

LONDON: HER MAJESTY'S STATIONERY OFFICE

© *Crown copyright 1975*
First published 1975

ISBN 0 11 340672 X

FOREWORD

In a previous report published in this Series (No. 15: *The Controlled Trial in Institutional Research*) the present authors drew on their experience at Kingswood Training School to argue that the limitations of the controlled trial as a method of evaluating residential treatment for delinquents have been given insufficient recognition. In particular, they considered that the results of such research were usually difficult to interpret because of the complexity of the situations being compared.

Despite weaknesses of the method, it was thought that the findings of the controlled trial undertaken at Kingswood merited publication. The study showed that the two regimes being compared—a 'therapeutic community' and a more traditional approved school approach—were equally ineffective in reducing the incidence of boys' delinquency, even though they were apparently dissimilar in respect of aims, of staff attitudes and policies, and of the boys' behaviour while at the school.

As well as indicating that a 'therapeutic community' in particular appears to offer no panacea for delinquency, the results provide further evidence of the seeming failure of residential methods to have any lasting effect on the rehabilitation of delinquents—although there may be other reasons for placing delinquents in residential institutions. In the latter part of the report, the authors attempt to provide some explanation for this failure; they argue that current approaches to the treatment of delinquents place too much emphasis upon trying to modify the deviant personalities or attitudes which are often presumed to underlie delinquency. They suggest that greater progress would be made if the importance were recognised first, of the offender's immediate environment in eliciting delinquent behaviour and second, of the learning process which establishes habitual responses to particular situations. Greater efforts might then be made to modify the particular circumstances in a child's home and in his wider social environment which have a bearing on delinquency.

July 1975

I J CROFT
Head of the Research Unit

ACKNOWLEDGEMENTS

The research described in this report was the result of close collaboration between Kingswood Schools and the Home Office Research Unit. The authors now work at the Unit, but both spent some time employed at Kingswood and it was while working there that, as the result of a request by the Principal and Managers of the Schools, one of them (RVGC) designed and initiated research into the effectiveness of a therapeutic community regime established in the training school by Mr J L Briers, the school's clinical psychologist.

We would like to thank the Managers, and Mr J L Burns the Principal, for their help and encouragement throughout the research. We are also grateful to the headmasters and staff of the schools for their co-operation and support during the long course of the work. Kingswood Foundation's agreement to publication, of course, does not necessarily commit them to all the views expressed in this volume.

R V G CLARKE
D B CORNISH

CONTENTS

		Page
Foreword		iii
Acknowledgements		iv

CHAPTER 1	INTRODUCTION	1
	Background to the research	2
	Research design	3
	The criterion of effectiveness	5

CHAPTER 2	THE REGIMES BEING COMPARED	7
	Setting and facilities	7
	The C House programme	8
	The E House programme	9
	Differences between houses in the attitudes of staff and the behaviour of boys	11

CHAPTER 3	FINDINGS	13
	Selection procedures	13
	The success of random allocation between E House and C House	16
	Results of the comparisons of long-term effectiveness	16

CHAPTER 4	AN ASSESSMENT OF THE FINDINGS	20
	Adequacy of implementation	20
	Adequacy of success criteria	22
	The relevance of reconviction	23

CHAPTER 5	THE RESULTS OF PREVIOUS EVALUATIVE RESEARCH	28
	Differential effectiveness of approved school regimes	28
	Other findings concerning differential effectiveness	29
	The overall effectiveness of institutional programmes	32
	Institutional versus non-institutional intervention	34

CHAPTER 6	EXPLAINING THE INEFFECTIVENESS OF RESIDENTIAL INTERVENTION	36
	The traditional model of intervention	36
	An alternative model of intervention	39
	Implications of the alternative model	42

CHAPTER 7	POSTSCRIPT—THE FUTURE ROLE OF INSTITUTIONS	46
	Their role in dealing with delinquents	46
	Their other functions with respect to delinquents	50

		Page
APPENDIX 1	Changes in the research design	52
APPENDIX 2	Differences between E and C Houses	55
APPENDIX 3	Staffs' own evaluation of their effectiveness	67
REFERENCES		69

CHAPTER 1

Introduction

This report discusses the extent to which residential placement is an effective means of dealing with delinquents. It begins by presenting the results of a controlled trial which compared two different methods of intervention* developed by Kingswood Training School, a residential institution for delinquent boys located near Bristol. This was formerly an approved school and is now a community home admitting boys between the ages of 13 and 15. The research was undertaken in two of the school's house units, one providing intervention along 'therapeutic community' lines, the other offering a more conventional approved school approach. The primary aim of residential intervention was defined by the research workers as being the reduction of the boys' subsequent delinquency, and for this reason various measures of post-institutional offending constituted the criteria of long-term effectiveness.

The research, which included a two-year follow-up period, spanned the years 1965–1973. Until 1971, when care orders under the Children and Young Persons Act 1969 replaced them, approved school orders (Children and Young Persons Act 1933) were the main means of dealing with offenders aged between 10 and 17 who were judged to need removal from home and fairly long residential placement (averaging 17 months for boys in 1970). Boys who were the subject of the study had all been dealt with under this earlier legislation.

The 1969 Act was designed to facilitate the integration of legal and social provisions for the care and control of children and, in particular, to minimise the distinctions previously made between delinquent and deprived children. This was to be achieved by providing a care jurisdiction covering all grounds on which a child under 17 who was in need of care and control might be brought before a juvenile court, by replacing the approved school order with a more general order committing the child to the care of a local authority, and by absorbing the approved schools into a comprehensive system of community homes available for all children in care. These changes at first appeared to make it more difficult to defend the criterion of effectiveness employed in this research (see Chapter 4). It became clear, however, that the relevance of the findings were in no way prejudiced by these developments. Despite the new legislation it seems unlikely that either the former approved schools or the kind of boys they receive will change greatly over the next few years (Gill, 1974). Moreover,

---

* In penology the term 'treatment' has gradually acquired a somewhat restricted and emotive meaning; it is, for example, often contrasted with 'training' or 'custody' (See Street et al., 1966, and its use elsewhere in the present report). Accordingly we have avoided its use as a generic term in favour of the more neutral term, 'intervention', since this makes no implicit prejudgments about the relative values of methods derived from different theoretical orientations.

whatever legislation is in force, it is still important to determine whether residential intervention is an effective means of dealing with children's delinquent behaviour.

Background to the research

In the years preceding their absorption into the community homes system, the approved schools were faced by apparently falling success rates as measured by the percentages of boys reconvicted after release. This lack of success was attributed to a decline in the quality of their intake and to the failure of traditional methods of intervention (see Chapter 4). As a result schools became increasingly receptive to methods based upon contemporary psychological theory. Individual psychotherapy was, however, an impractical proposition for the schools: psychiatrists with sufficient skill and experience in dealing with delinquents were scarce, the method was expensive and the boys were often unco-operative and unsuitable. Psychotherapeutic methods which involved working with groups rather than with individuals seemed to be more relevant in the institutional context, and these were being developed both by Bion (1961) at Northfield Military Hospital and Maxwell Jones (1952) at the Henderson Hospital (Belmont). It was the examples of these innovators, together with those of pioneers in residential work with maladjusted children (see Bridgeland, 1971, for a comprehensive survey) which provided the approved schools with a more appropriate framework within which to employ psychotherapeutic techniques. Kingswood Training School was the first* approved school to make a determined effort to implement these methods; the school was already divided into three separate house units and in 1954 a clinical psychologist was appointed who began to develop group work within the houses. Once this was established as a regular part of the school programme he suggested that a 'therapeutic community' should be set up in one of the houses. In 1964 the house with the most successful experience of group work was selected for the experiment.

As the result of a decision by the Managers of Kingswood Schools it was agreed that an attempt should be made to evaluate the effectiveness of the 'therapeutic community' by comparing it with the more orthodox approved school training offered by one of the two other houses. The specific question asked was whether 'training' or 'treatment' was the more suitable method for rehabilitating the particular sub-section of the approved school population which was thought to include the more maladjusted boys. The term 'training' was held to imply the belief that delinquents have most need of training in social, educational and vocational skills, whereas 'treatment' implied the belief that they were most in need of the diagnosis and treatment of underlying problems of personal and interpersonal adjustment.

---

* Similar work had, of course, been done in 'The Little Commonwealth', which received a short-lived certificate of approval in 1917, and in the Caldecott Community (Rendel, 1959) but these are outside the mainstream of approved school work.

INTRODUCTION

Research design

The eventual form of the research design was as follows: from the pool of 280 boys allocated between August 1965 and October 1969 to Kingswood Training School (mainly from the regional classifying school*) the staff of the Experimental (E) House selected those (N=173) whom they considered would benefit from the treatment offered by their therapeutic community. These eligible boys were then randomly allocated between the E House (N=86) and the Control (C) House (N=87) so as to ensure that any differences in outcome could be reliably assigned to differences in the respective methods employed by the two houses, rather than to differences between the groups of boys entering the two houses. Boys considered ineligible (N=107) did not take part in the controlled trial, but entered the school's Third House (see diagram). After leaving the school each boy was followed up through official records for a period of two years in order to obtain information about any further convictions.

The mean age of the 280 boys who took part in the research was 14·3 years. Their mean IQ was 104·5 and they showed considerable reading retardation, their mean reading age being 10·5 years. There was no question of their delinquent status—they averaged 3·1 previous court appearances.

The design of the controlled trial had originally been somewhat more rigorous and in Appendix 1 the important changes made to the design and the reasons for them are discussed. At this juncture it need only be mentioned that this resulted in abandoning a lengthy programme to test the personalities and attitudes of boys, both before they entered the school and when they were on the point of leaving. The time spent on describing and measuring aspects of the regimes being compared was also heavily curtailed. Though these changes seem to represent considerable departures from the original plan, it will become apparent from the discussion later in the paper that neither are considered to weaken the main conclusions of the research.

It should further be noted that the controlled trial was not undertaken with the intention of comparing the effectiveness with which two different programmes could deal with the general run of approved schoolboys. Indeed research of the time suggested the existence of interactions between types of delinquents and types of programmes such that particular programmes might be most effective with certain kinds of boys. Bearing this in mind, it was thought that the most powerful and economic test of the effectiveness of the Kingswood therapeutic community would be a research design which, by allowing the regime to select the boys with whom it preferred to deal, maximised its chances of success when compared with a more traditional type of programme admitting a similar group of boys. This form of design has certain implications for the interpretation of results. If, for example, the C House were shown to be less effective than the E

---

* This classifying school, which served the South West of England and Wales, was on the same estate as Kingswood Training School. The 280 boys allocated to the latter included a few sent from other classifying schools.

RESIDENTIAL TREATMENT AND ITS EFFECTS ON DELINQUENCY

THE ALLOCATION OF BOYS TO HOUSES DURING THE CONTROLLED TRIAL

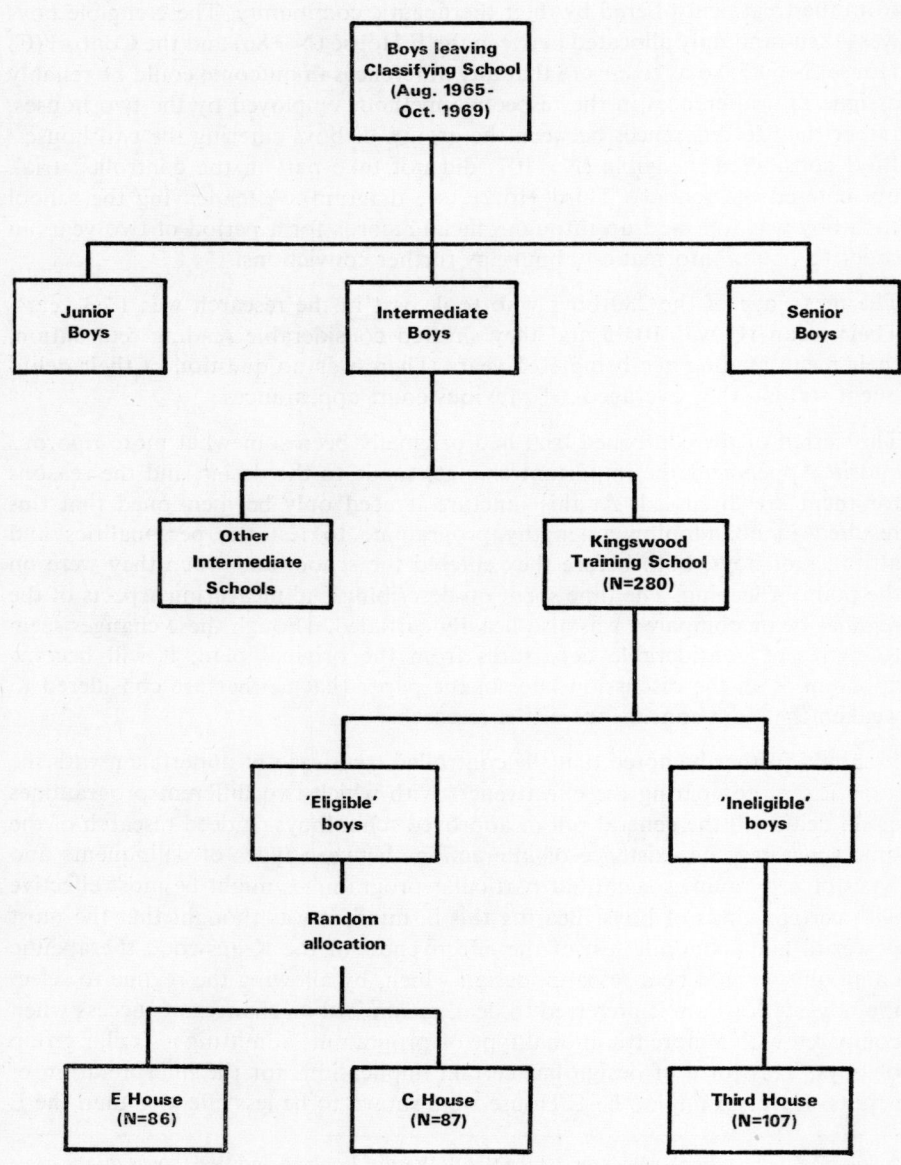

House, the former could still object that this merely reflected its relative inability to deal with boys whom it would not ordinarily attempt to treat, and in this sense claim that its methods were not fully on trial. If, on the other hand, the therapeutic community failed to produce better results than the C House, even when ostensibly able to maximise its potential effectiveness by using a favourable selection policy, it would be unlikely that the method could under any circumstances be more effective than traditional programmes.

The difficulties of carrying out controlled trials in institutional settings were evaluated in a previous paper (Clarke & Cornish, 1972). It was argued that this type of research design is usually an inefficient and expensive way of obtaining information and also that the results in many cases may be difficult to interpret. This is particularly likely to be true when the intervention programmes differ both in their methods and in the extent to which they are subsequently effective in reducing delinquent behaviour since, because of the large numbers of programme variables involved—any one or combination of which might have contributed to outcome—causes and effects can rarely be linked unambiguously. Where, as in the present research, identifiably different programmes result in similar outcomes, the question ceases to be one of trying to determine which programme variables influenced outcomes and becomes one of finding out why these variables had so little differential effect. An attempt to answer this latter question is made in Chapter 6.

The first paper also discussed the problem of generalising from results; in the present research generalisation was limited by the unique natures of the regimes and by their setting, but some compensation was made for this by comparing the findings with those obtained from other similar regimes running in approved schools and, more generally, with the results of other research (see Chapter 5).

The criterion of effectiveness

The use of reconviction data in assessing the long-term effectiveness of institutional programmes will be discussed at some length in Chapter 4; at this point discussion will be limited to explaining why the reduction of delinquency was selected in this research as representing the main aim of approved school work. The decision arose out of a consideration of the grounds upon which boys were sent to approved schools. It appeared that there were basically three categories of boy:

- (a) Those who were delinquent. These had usually committed offences involving theft and constitute, even in 1975, by far the largest group in the schools. In 1970—the last year for which statistics were produced—offenders made up 96% of the admissions to all boys' approved schools (HMSO, 1972);
- (b) Those primarily in need of substitute care;
- (c) Those in need of compulsory education (in 1970 about 2% fell into this category).

Even these categories (particularly the first two) are not as distinct as the grounds for committal might indicate. In practically all cases, the main problem leading to committal was delinquent behaviour and it thus appears reasonable to describe the primary functions of the schools as being the immediate control and long-term reduction of delinquency; for a very small minority substitute care and education may assume greater importance.

Where other aims have been claimed by practitioners, this has often resulted from a confusion of ends with means. The reduction of delinquent behaviour can, for all practical purposes, only be tackled indirectly by the schools, and for this reason all sorts of 'intermediate aims' have been put forward in the hope that their achievement will affect post-institutional offending. Thus some schools have emphasized trade-training or education, others the reduction of apparent maladjustment by trying to change attitudes or improve interpersonal skills. The extent to which these intermediate aims are realised, however, is of secondary interest unless it is clear that they relate to the reduction of delinquency.

CHAPTER 2

The Regimes Being Compared

Setting and facilities

The three house units of Kingswood Training School form parts of a single building of late nineteenth century design constructed around three sides of a quadrangle. By the time that the experimental programme was established, in 1964, the houses were functioning as substantially self-contained units with some measure of administrative autonomy. As the main interest of the research is in the comparison of the E and C Houses, only such information about the Third House as is needed for an understanding of the project is given in this report.

Although the E and C Houses were adjacent, communication between them had to take place by means of their front entrances. Each house had its own bedrooms, washing facilities, day rooms and tuck shops, but classrooms, assembly hall, trade departments, playing areas and sick bay were shared. The dining room was also shared, but separate areas were partitioned-off for each house. The senior staff and also the staff of the E House had always been anxious to extend the separation of living arrangements to include eating facilities, and eventually to completely separate buildings, but financial difficulties had prevented this.

In common with all approved schools, teachers and instructors at Kingswood were attached to particular houses for supervising the boys when full-time house staff were off duty. While these 'extraneous duties' staff were fully integrated into their respective house programmes, they could also find themselves teaching boys from other houses during the course of the school day. Senior staff also carried out supervisory duties in the school at certain times, and the extent to which these circumstances affected the adequacy with which the programme was implemented will be discussed later in the report.

As well as being educated and trained in the company of boys from other houses, boys met together for morning assembly and for pre-school parades, though at these times they remained in their house groups. Many evening recreations such as snooker, table-tennis, and television, took place within the houses, but some other activities such as model-building, pottery and the boys' club were provided on a school, not house, basis. Many of these, however, were not regular features of the school timetable.

Though the premises occupied by the E and C Houses were very similar, visitors throughout the course of the experiment commented on the marked difference in their physical condition. The C House was comfortable, homely and well-furnished, and the atmosphere was that of a tidy well-maintained private house with a place for everything and everything in its place. A number of factors contributed to this: the stability of the house (see below), which had enabled material gains to be consolidated over the years; considerable contributions to the house funds (£130 in 1964) by way of the house's garden, tuck-shop and hens; and a system of fines and incentives, geared towards maintaining acceptable standards of behaviour and keeping the house in good condition. Senior staff, managers, official visitors, and the research workers themselves were immediately struck, however, by the bareness, untidiness and frequently dilapidated state of the fixtures and fittings in the E House. Again there were many contributing factors: there was for a long period no permanent housemother who might have seen the physical state of the house as a reflection on her work; the staff as a group felt that too much attention was paid in approved schools to 'spit-and-polish' and not enough to the boys themselves; and any decisions about improving the condition of the house had to be taken in collaboration with the boys who, like most boys, were unlikely to be particularly concerned about such matters.

The poor impression made by the physical appearance of the house contributed to the difficulties experienced by the house team in maintaining support for the continuation of the experimental regime. Senior staff, for example, though unwilling to infringe on the autonomy of the House, felt that their tasks of giving it support and of answering criticisms from outside the school were made unnecessarily difficult by the lack of attention paid by staff and boys to these matters.

The C House programme

The C House was selected as a control, firstly, because the husband-and-wife team of housemaster and housemother had been running the House for the ten years preceding the establishment of the therapeutic community. This, in contrast with the position in the Third House, meant that the regime was securely established with clearly defined features. Secondly, the housemaster and his wife were convinced that their methods were successful and were eager to take part in the controlled trial and, thirdly, group work had not been developed to any great extent in the C House, which relied on the more 'traditional' methods of individual casework when attempting to deal with boys' underlying problems.

Care of the physical surroundings was only one element in the C House programme. It also emphasized the traditional approved school ingredients of a structured environment, a clearly defined system of rewards and punishments based on extrinsic motivation, and a belief in the importance of habit training and character development through obedience. In a report to the Managers made in 1964 the C housemaster described the aims of the House in these terms:

'The purpose of our work is to establish and maintain a community based on the Christian Ethic, in which a deprived, maladjusted delinquent boy may, through precept, example and experience, assimilate a scale of values which will enable him to live at peace with himself, in harmony with his family, and in conformity with society . . . This, we feel . . . is proceeding steadily and quietly.'

Since the housemaster and his wife were the only full-time house staff, decisions tended to be taken by them about house-matters, about boys' behaviour, and about rules and regulations. Responsibility for action on matters connected with the boys' homes and arrangements for after-care also rested largely with the housemaster, and during much of the research other staff who undertook duties in the house had little to do with the boys' files and little knowledge of what was in them.

Relations between boys and staff were usually friendly and the regime may be characterised as benevolently paternalistic but cautiously liberal in its outlook.

The E House programme

As Zeitlyn (1967) points out, discussion of therapeutic communities is often hindered by the imprecision with which the term is defined; even when applied to treatment designed for the mentally-ill, usage of the term varies from description of comparatively limited changes in traditional mental hospital structure to far-reaching alterations in both milieu and in patient-staff relationships. The label 'therapeutic community' for the E House (and also later for some other approved school regimes) was applied in an even less well-defined fashion, as a catch-all to denote the borrowing of innovations, not just from the psychiatric field, but also from such diverse fields as progressive education, the psychoanalytic treatment of delinquents and the work of schools for the maladjusted.

To these influences on the form the therapeutic community took at Kingswood must be added three further constraints which may have affected the direction of the development of the experimental regime. Firstly, less freedom for experiment is available in institutions which have clearly defined statutory duties in the areas of education, health and welfare, than in many privately-run ventures. Moreover, each individual institution, as well as carrying out these duties, evolves its own customary ways of operating in these and other areas of residential life. These 'traditions' place further limitations upon the freedom to experiment. Lastly, many of those working with adolescents have commented on the need for staff to be more directive in their approach than would be the case with adults (Jones, 1960; Martin, 1962; Wills, 1941). Because of these factors, the E House was sometimes referred to in Kingwood's internal memoranda as a 'modified', rather than a fully-fledged, therapeutic community.

The principles and methods of the E House were very fully discussed in various reports made to the Managers of Kingswood Schools* by Mr J Briers, the clinical psychologist who established the regime; following Rapoport (1960), he outlined the four principles which underpinned the E House programme:

(a) Democratization: this is characterized by the flattening of the conventional staff hierarchy, and the egalitarian participation by staff and boys in

---

* In this section, in the following chapter and in Appendix II, use has been made of various reports prepared for the Managers by Mr Briers, other staff of the E House, and headmasters of the Training School.

making decisions about house matters ('shared responsibility'), both administrative and therapeutic.
(b) Communalism: this encourages the development of an informal atmosphere to facilitate communication between staff and boys—signified, for example, by the using of first names by all, the abandonment of an office or special staff room in the house, and some sharing of domestic duties.
(c) Permissiveness: this is characterized by the toleration of a wide measure of deviant behaviour to allow 'acting out'.
(d) Reality confrontation: this involves the continual communication to members of the ways in which other people interpret their behaviour. To serve the same purpose, the need is stressed for interaction between the house and the outside community.

Group meetings were seen by the E House staff as the single most important component in the intervention process, as shown by the following extract from a report made by the clinical psychologist:

'One of the principal aims of group work in an approved school is the use of a social situation to help the individual to internalise the codes and values acceptable to a normal society. More particularly, one can see this as the aim of the group-centred community, the community in which all members are able to participate in the experience of shared responsibility. Also, one of the ways of overcoming the ambivalence and hostility found amongst so many children in institutional care is to give them a feeling of belonging and acceptance, even if they break the rules of the school. If this is to be done much depends on the climate of the school or unit, and here shared responsibility is important. Warmth and acceptance will help to encourage trust and confidence, but shared responsibility and community decision-making will help to foster independent thinking and initiative, two qualities important to the boy who needs to internalise non-delinquent and acceptable standards of behaviour'.

Attempts were made to extend the influence of group work to every facet of day-to-day living in the unit. Groups varied in size, and the group work varied in its level of therapeutic intensity according to circumstances. The largest group, which consisted of all boys in the house and those of its staff who were on duty, met twice on each weekday, morning and afternoon*. A chairman and a secretary were elected by the group, and although attendance was voluntary, it was exceptional for more than one or two members to be absent on any one occasion.

The main purpose of these meetings was to discuss various aspects of the community's life, to solve the problems of living together and to adjudicate on disputes. This kind of group activity has been described by Jones (1960) as social

---

* Impromptu meetings were often held in addition to these twice-daily meetings when events in the house made it necessary; these could be called by staff or boys.

therapy, since it is concerned mainly with practical problem solving and learning to live harmoniously with peers and adults, rather than with more fundamental problems of personal adjustment. Each day there was also a meeting of staff to discuss problems or information which had come to light at meetings with the boys; attempts were made to ensure that communication at these staff meetings was as free as possible so that the cohesiveness of the staff team could be maintained in the face of attempted manipulation by the boys and of the occasionally inevitable clashes of opinion amongst staff about intervention policy.

Smaller groups of five or six boys met once or twice a week for other purposes; during 1968, for example, small groups were in operation for new boys, for group counselling sessions, and for awarding leave passes to individual members of the house. These small groups made it possible to examine more fully the interpersonal problems that the boys had with their peers, members of staff, and their parents, and it was here that group therapeutic techniques were most closely approached. While these sessions were always guided to some extent by psychodynamic theory, the way in which the staff tackled a problem, particularly after the departure of the clinical psychologist, tended to become of a more pragmatic or counselling nature. Although individual contacts between staff and boys were not discouraged, it was felt that since many of the boys' difficulties were in the areas of interpersonal relationships and communal living, these were best discussed in a group setting.

Attempts were also made to utilize the therapeutic potential of other aspects of house life; for instance, staff helped in the daily domestic cleaning duties alongside the boys, and instead of boys being allotted one particular duty (as was often the case in the two other houses), members were organized into cleaning groups with special areas of responsibility. Although there is always the danger that drudgery will masquerade as therapy (Zeitlyn, 1967; Rapoport, 1960), the E House tried to avoid this by using the cleaning groups as weekly leave pass discussion groups so that applications from members for weekend leave passes (called 'privilege' leave by the school, to distinguish it from longer home leave) could be discussed among those who knew the boy and his behaviour best.

Differences between houses in the attitudes of staff and the behaviour of boys

It was clearly important to determine whether the readily observable differences in the 'form' of the regimes were matched by differences of 'content', as reflected in the attitudes of staff and the policies they pursued over particular issues, as well as in the behaviour of the boys. Only with information of this kind would it be possible to make some attempt at interpretation of any subsequent findings. The work concerned with identifying differences in the regimes was one of the main casualties of the decision to limit the scale of the project as a whole. Despite this, it proved possible to examine data from a wide variety of sources during the course of the research, including:

    (a) staff records;

(b) two specially designed questionnaires to examine the general attitudes of staff to dealing with delinquents and their policies concerning particular issues;
(c) observation of house practice with respect to such matters as the allocation of leave, pocket money, and domestic duties;
(d) a log of visits to the house and of contacts with the boys' homes;
(e) records of damage to furniture and fittings as well as of repairs to clothing;
(f) enuresis records;
(g) absconding and punishment records, and records of offences committed during the boys' stay at Kingswood;
(h) sociometry;
(i) staff ratings of boys' response to training; and
(j) a questionnaire to assess the boys' view of the regimes.

Many differences were found; these are summarised below and are described in detail in Appendix 2.

Throughout the course of the research and before, there had been a policy of employing staff who would be sympathetic to the regime in which they would be expected to work. This policy resulted in differences in age, qualifications, and experience between the staff in the two houses, those in the E House being younger and more likely to have professionally-qualified child care or social work backgrounds, while those in the C House were more likely to have teaching qualifications.

These differences in background were reflected in a more consistent and stronger 'treatment' (as against 'training') orientation amongst E House staff, both in general attitudes to dealing with delinquents and over more specific matters of house policy.

These differences were in turn reflected in the handling of such matters as the allocation of domestic duties, the 'style' of social interaction between staff and boys, the granting of 'privilege' and home leaves, the allocation of pocket money, the use of corporal punishment, and the punishment of absconding. There was also some evidence that the E House policies fostered greater contact between boys, their parents, and after-care officers during the programme.

The differences in regimes were evident to the boys in the two houses and there were some differences in behaviour between them. For instance, the boys in the C House were less likely to 'act out' by absconding or by damaging furniture and the fabric of the house. On the other hand, there was no difference between the two houses in the amount of offending which took place during the boys' stay. Moreover, boys in both houses appeared to be equally contented, their friendship patterns were similar, and there was little evidence that in either house they were known better by the staff or had better relationships with them.

CHAPTER 3

Findings

Selection procedures

It was considered essential that the E House staff should be responsible for determining the eligibility of boys admitted to the therapeutic community. There were three reasons for this: (1) a selection system imposed from without might have had harmful effects upon staff morale and might have been represented as undermining the whole philosophy of the regime; (2) the staff responsible for implementing the regime were thought to be in the best position to determine eligibility; and (3) previous work in therapeutic communities had indicated that it is desirable to keep intake policy flexible so that it can vary to take account of the composition of the existing inmate group.

Descriptions by E House staff of the factors they tried to take into account when determining eligibility* are contained in two documents produced during the course of the research. In the early days of the E House only general guidelines were laid down for selection. The presence of emotional or social maladjustment was considered of prime importance, the clinical psychologist commenting that where facilities were limited there would be little point in selecting well-adjusted individuals for admission to a therapeutic community. Second, it was thought that only those who were of a personality type likely to be responsive to the therapeutic community's environment should be admitted. In this context it was considered that, (1) intellectual dullness, especially when combined with 'social dullness', (2) weak ego-control, defined as 'immature personality', and (3) indications of extrapunitive attitudes, would all serve to render candidates ineligible. Later in the project the Principal, in an attempt to broaden the basis for selection (see Appendix 1), asked the house team to define their admission criteria more clearly and in January 1968 the following major factors that debarred admission were outlined:

Full scale IQ (Wechsler Intelligence Scale for Children) 90 or below;
Mental illness—indications of withdrawal over a long period;
Inability to form meaningful relationships, accompanied by an inability to learn from experience and to show concern and anxiety;
Behaviour so excessive, aggressive or destructive, as to endanger the stability of the House.

The earlier and later criteria for selection had much in common, and it was hoped that an analysis of background information for each boy would give some indication of the relative importance of these criteria.

---

* During the early part of the controlled trial boys might be interviewed by a member of the E House staff before a decision as to eligibility was made, but this practice was largely discontinued after the clinical psychologist left and decisions were based solely on the boys' Assessment Centre reports.

Information was collected for the whole intake to the training school under the following heads*:

(1) home circumstances;
(2) number of siblings;
(3) criminal record of parents;
(4) criminal record of siblings;
(5) mental illness in family;
(6) boy ever in care;
(7) siblings ever in care;
(8) number of court appearances;
(9) age at first court appearance;
(10) months elapsing between court appearances;
(11) number of approved schools previously attended;
(12) previous psychiatric investigation;
(13) history of absconding;
(14) IQ;
(15) height;
(16) weight;
(17) age;
(18) social class;
(19) reading age.

Comparisons between the *eligible* and *ineligible* groups revealed differences only with respect to three of the nineteen factors:

(1) The ineligible group were significantly less intelligent (mean IQ 91·4) than the eligibles (mean IQ 104·5) as measured by the Wechsler Intelligence Scale for children ($t=8·24$, $p<·001$).† Only 13 of the 173 boys in the 'eligible' group obtained IQ scores of less than 90.
(2) The mean reading age (Burt (Rearranged) Word Reading Test) for the eligibles was 10·5 years while for the ineligibles it was 9·1 years ($t=6·3$, $p<·001$). Reading age is, of course, to some extent associated with intelligence.
(3) Rather more ineligibles came from very large families; for instance, 24·3% of ineligibles came from families of eight or more children as against 11·6% of the eligibles (chi-square, on a division into six approximately equal categories, was 11·10, $p<·05$).

A more complex analysis was also performed on the data, using the AID (Automatic Interaction Detector) programme (Sonquist, 1970), a technique for examining the relationships among a set of variables. One of the variables—in this case eligibility/ineligibility for the E House—is used as the dependent variable and the analysis proceeds by the way of a non-symmetrical branching

---

* Information was originally collected on a number of further variables but this was discarded early in the research.
† All tests of significance reported in this paper are two-tailed.

process, based on analysis of variance techniques, to subdivide the sample into a series of subgroups which maximises the ability to predict the dependent variable. Although used in our case upon a smaller than desirable sample, the analysis confirmed that IQ was the main predictor of membership of the eligible group; but even IQ explained only about 21% of the variance. Other variables were of little predictive value.

At this point it was clear that, so far as could be discovered from our statistical analysis, the eligible and ineligible groups appeared to differ little except in terms of intelligence, reading age and family size. As such the results provide some evidence that staff were using IQ as a major selection criterion. As far as their other criteria are concerned, however, the statistical analysis offers little direct support for their importance. But for most of the nineteen background variables a case could have been made for describing their influence as favourable or adverse with regard to some general criterion such as 'treatment amenability'. No attempt was made to construct scales using these variables, though it was found that on sixteen of the latter the ineligible group tended to be less favourably situated than the eligible. The consistent direction of the trend raises the possibility that E House staff may sometimes have tightened up selection procedures as circumstances within the house dictated, in order to avoid adding to temporary difficulties by admitting less amenable boys; Rapoport (1960) describes how oscillation in a therapeutic community's affairs may lead to such changes in selection procedures. In 1968, for example, it was found that for boys in the school at that time the ineligible group had a history of more admissions to the care of a local authority than the eligible group, in addition to the other significant differences between the two groups mentioned above.

The E House selection procedure had affinities with those of similar regimes. This suggests that as long as current experiments in residential intervention emphasise the importance of group work and verbal interaction, their staff will prefer, where practicable, to admit the more intelligent delinquent. Jones (1960) notes that maladjusted boys admitted to "Woodmarsh" were required to be of at least average intelligence; Franklin (1966) remarks that only in special circumstances were those with IQ scores below 86 accepted for "Q-Camps"; while Loaningdale, a Scottish approved school (see Chapter 5), restricted its admissions to those with IQ scores above 90 (McMichael, 1972). Experimental projects tend to operate cautious selection procedures in order to place the results of the new techniques in the best possible light, especially where 'permissive' methods expose those involved to the possibility of public criticism. There is little evidence, however, that the more intelligent delinquents present substantially better risks or are either easier or pleasanter to deal with than duller boys*, although Sinclair & Clarke (1973) found that of the 66 approved schools they studied those admitting the more intelligent boys tended to have the better success-rates.

---

* For our total sample (N=280) the likelihood of reconviction was not found to be related to IQ.

The success of random allocation between E House and C House

Because of the relatively small numbers and rather crude technique of random allocation which was used, it was necessary to discover whether, in fact, the random allocation had worked. Comparison of the two groups on the nineteen background factors for which information was collected revealed no significant differences—an indication that random allocation had successfully ensured the similarity of the groups entering the E and C Houses.

Random allocation can ensure equivalence only at the outset of a controlled trial, and bias may subsequently be introduced as a result of differential attrition of the groups. During the course of the experiment 17 boys from the C House and 16 boys from the E House failed to complete their stay at the school. These boys were either transferred to other approved schools or had their stay terminated by a further court order* (see Table 1). No significant difference was found in the average time that E and C failures spent in their respective houses, though this might have been expected given other differences in house policies†. Because of the small and equal numbers involved these boys are included in most analyses, except for some relating to reconviction.

Results of the comparisons of long-term effectiveness

The criterion selected to determine the effectiveness of the two methods under study was that of subsequent convictions (as recorded in the Criminal Records Office) for a two-year period immediately following the boy's stay in the school.

The percentages of those admitted to each house who were reconvicted during this period are given in column (c) of Table 1; there were no significant differences either between E and C Houses, or between these two and the Third House.

Table 1

HOUSE	(a) N admitted	(b) N reconvicted	(c) % reconvicted	(d) N failing to complete stay at Kingswood	(e) N released on aftercare	(f) N reconvicted of those released on aftercare	(g) % reconvicted of those released on aftercare*	(h) Composite failure rate (columns d+f)
E	86	60	70%	16	70	47	67%	73%
C	87	60	69%	17	70	45	64%	71%
Third	107	73	68%	35	72	49	68%	79%
Totals	280	193	69%	68	212	141	67%	75%

* Figures in this column cannot be compared directly with the reconviction figures made available for the whole approved school population by official sources; official success rates are based on a longer follow-up (three years) but also, as we discovered, on less complete information about subsequent offending.

---

* All but two of the latter also went straight on to other approved schools or to borstal training.
† Appendix 2 presents evidence that the E House was somewhat more tolerant of persistent absconders than the C House, and kept them for longer periods before transferring them to other schools.

It is felt that results based on reconviction data for all the boys *admitted* (Table 1 columns b and c) constitute a more accurate criterion of the effectiveness of institutional intervention than ones based only on those who were *released on after-care* from Kingswood (columns f and g). Programmes may look more successful than they really are simply because potential failures have been culled; in the present sample those who failed to complete their stay (column d) tended to have rather higher reconviction rates (76%) than those who were released in the ordinary way (67%). This was despite the fact that, since 64 out of the 68 boys who left prematurely went straight on to a further period of institutional intervention at either another approved school or borstal, they presumably had less opportunity during their follow-up period to commit further offences than did those released in the ordinary way. While there was no evidence in the controlled trial of unilateral attempts by E or C programmes to improve their success-rates by culling, the success-rates for both show equal, though small, improvement when only those released on after-care are considered (column g).*

But even the reconviction figures given in column (b) may underestimate the real position. It was mentioned above that boys leaving Kingswood prematurely (column d) ran less risk of being reconvicted during the two-year follow-up period. This, combined with the fact that CRO records on juveniles—though the best source of readily-available information on delinquent behaviour—tend to be less comprehensive than those on adults, leads to the suspicion that our reconviction figures still overstate the effectiveness of all three houses in reducing delinquent behaviour in the long term.

There are also unresolved questions about the real size of the successful group. A two-year follow-up period was chosen for the present research because it seemed, from evidence of previous research, to provide an adequate time-span over which to evaluate institutional effectiveness; this question is discussed further in the next chapter. It was also felt that the adoption of the standard two-year period would enable analysis of the data to proceed within a reasonable period of the last boy's departure from his institutional programme. Since the time-span of the research was long, however, reconviction data for a substantial proportion of the sample are available for a longer period. For example, of the overall successes (N=87) 30 committed offences after the end of their two-year follow-up period.† This suggests that only for about 20% of those admitted to the school could it be argued that institutional intervention had provided more than a temporary interruption of their delinquent behaviour.

---

* Significantly fewer boys entering the Third House completed their stay at Kingswood (chi-square=5·96; d.f.1, p<·025). This, together with the fact that significantly more boys from the Third House than from the other two houses committed offences while at Kingswood (see Appendix II), may reflect the management problems suffered by the Third House during the research (Clarke & Cornish, 1972). There was, as we have seen, little evidence that boys entering this house had a significantly greater prior likelihood of reconviction than the eligible group.
† Proportions committing offences were similar for each of the three houses.

These last results will be referred to again when, in Chapter Five, we examine the effectiveness of institutional programmes in absolute terms. As far as relative success-rates are concerned, it can be seen that no differences existed between the E and C Houses, whether the criterion of success employed was liberal or more stringent. Perhaps the most satisfactory (though most rigorous) criterion of programme effectiveness would be one which reflected both the drop-out rate, and reconviction-rates of those released on after-care. In this way some weight could be given to a programme's success at coping with those allocated to it, as well as its success with those it was able to retain. Column (h) presents this composite failure rate for all three houses.

Since reconviction rates are sometimes criticised for being relatively insensitive measures of subsequent delinquency, some simple refinements were introduced. For those boys who completed their programme (N=212), the following indices were calculated: time to first conviction after release, number of subsequent court appearances, proportion of custodial disposals, and the 'seriousness' of the first offence after release. It proved impossible to use the sophisticated Sellin–Wolfgang index or its derivations (see Scott, 1964) because of the limited information available from criminal records. Instead, a score for each boy was derived by asking five members of approved schools staff* to rate on a five-point scale the 'seriousness' of the offence involved in the conviction following release. Some attempt was made to standardize the information available for each offence and the details of these—which usually included a description of the offence and (where applicable) of the modus operandi and value of goods stolen—were presented to each rater; but the identities of boys and the house they had been in were concealed, and no details were given of the court attended or the sentence awarded.

The results of these comparisons are set out in Table 2. There were no statistically significant differences between the E and C Houses on any of the measures; nor were there any differences between these two houses taken together and the Third House. Comparisons between the Third House and the E House revealed, however, that significantly more of the boys reconvicted after release from the former received custodial disposals. (Table 2, columns (e) and (f)). The disposal awarded might, of course, have been influenced by any reports made to the court by the school, as well as by other factors, such as previous criminal record (including amount of previous residential intervention) and age of offender. It is for this reason that the ratings of offence seriousness (column g) may provide a more accurate assessment.

More complex analyses using the AID programme described earlier, with 'reconvicted/ not reconvicted' as the dependent variable, produced essentially similar findings. A number of analyses were made on the total sample, the first of which used only the nineteen background factors referred to previously,

---

* Approved school staff were used as judges because they are amongst the most critical of the alleged insensitivity of reconviction rates.

FINDINGS

Table 2

HOUSE	(a) N released	(b) N Reconvicted	(c) Mean time to first conviction (in months)	(d) Mean number of court appearances	(e) Number of boys given custodial disposals	(f) % custodial disposals	(g) Mean 'seriousness' of first offence
E	70	47	12·0 (s.d.=5·7)	2·0	19	40·4%	2·9 (s.d.=0·9)
C	70	45	10·8 (s.d.=6·0)	1·9	25	55·6%	2·9 (s.d.=0·9)
Third	72	49	10·7 (s.d.=5·9)	2·1	32	65·3%	3·0 (s.d.=0·8)

together with information on which House each boy entered. The results confirmed that while such background factors as, for example, previous history of absconding or of attendance at approved schools, number of court appearances, and interval between offences, had some small predictive value with regard to the likelihood of subsequent reconviction, the house which a boy had entered had no influence. In a second analysis, only those factors related to the residential situation itself—house entered, number of days leave, total number of leave periods, absconding record at the school, length of stay in the school—were used. The results indicated that none of these variables had any significant effect on reconviction.

As a further check, other analyses were carried out using MCA (Multiple Classification Analysis), a multiple regression programme for use with categorical variables which relates a number of predictor variables to a dependent variable in the context of an additive model (Sonquist, 1970). Three regressions were performed, the first using the best four predictors from the AID analysis, the second using these plus the variable 'house entered', the third using the best seven predictors plus 'house entered'. In all cases multiple correlation coefficients were very low.

On the face of it, the results of the controlled trial seem to indicate that although the methods and policies of the therapeutic community and C House programmes differed in many respects their long-term effectiveness in reducing delinquent behaviour was virtually identical. It was earlier pointed out that since the E House was able to choose those boys who took part in the experiment proponents of therapeutic community methods would find such results especially difficult to discount. Two possible grounds upon which the research findings might be criticised are discussed in Chapter 4. Whatever the implications for the particular methods under investigation, however, the findings suggest in general that even specially tailored programmes may not increase the effectiveness of residential institutions in reducing delinquency. This, it will be shown later, raises fundamental questions about their usefulness.

CHAPTER 4

An Assessment of the Findings

For the group of boys under consideration the findings of the controlled trial appeared to indicate that, while marked differences existed between the houses and their programmes, these had no differential effect on the subsequent offending of the boys. Before accepting this conclusion, however, a number of objections must be dealt with. One main group of these concerns the adequacy with which the E House programme was implemented, the other, the adequacy with which effectiveness was measured.

Adequacy of implementation

The programme carried out at Kingswood was modelled largely on the Henderson Hospital's therapeutic community, and the E House's extensive programme of group work more than adequately reproduced similar work undertaken there. Even so, it might be objected that the amount of time (about 2–3 hours daily) devoted to formal therapeutic tasks was rather low. Apart from these times, the other occasions during the day when the E House boys were together, but separated from the rest of the school, were during the morning from 7.00 to 9.00 a.m., for a quarter-of-an-hour at mid-morning, at lunch (for one hour), and from 5.30 p.m. onwards. Much of this time was taken up with domestic work inside the house, with eating and with recreation.

Elsewhere (Cornish, 1973) it has been argued that one of the problems of running experimental programmes in residential settings is that there are always strict limitations on the amount of therapy which can take place; residential living tends to impose a relatively restricting time-table determined by the physical, educational and recreational needs of the inmates. Many of the things a boy is required or needs to do while living in a residential institution have little to do with his rehabilitation. Though some of these activities may provide an occasion for therapeutic intervention, this is not their primary function and their recruitment to the therapeutic enterprise requires more than an expression of intent on the part of those running a programme. It is perhaps more accurate to describe even sophisticated programmes as maintaining 'therapeutic islands' (Jesness et al., 1972), visited a few times per day, rather than as exerting a uniform and pervasive influence at all times.

One area, in particular, in which the E House may have suffered some disadvantage as compared with a therapeutic community working under ideal circumstances has already been mentioned. The periods spent outside the house in classrooms and trade departments were not only lost as occasions for direct therapy, but it is possible that they also exposed boys to the criticism and—in terms of the E House programme—inconsistent demands of the school's other staff, whose attitudes to dealing with delinquents (see Appendix 2) were less 'treatment' orientated. E House staff made the best of this state of affairs by treating it as experience of 'reality confrontation' (see Chapter 2). For such experience to be properly effective, however, the process would need to be regulated to suit the progress of individual boys, and would enlist the aid only of staff who were not connected with the E or C House programmes.

This incomplete insulation from the reactions of those outside the therapeutic community is one of the prices which have to be paid for reducing over-heads by sharing facilities.* To what extent the effectiveness of the E House was limited by its setting within a traditional approved school was an issue that frequently arose during the course of the project. It was only later in the research, when two nearby approved schools catering for the same age group began to operate as self-contained 'therapeutic communities' (see Millham et al., 1975), that there was an opportunity to shed some empirical light on the question. The two-year reconviction rates of the two groups of boys admitted to these schools in 1968 were found to be 68·3% (N=60) and 67·9% (N=53) respectively; these rates were not significantly different from those of the three houses at Kingswood. The intake groups were found to be similar to those of Kingswood on two of the three background variables examined (number of previous court appearances and age), but of significantly lower intelligence than the 'eligible' group (mean IQ 95·6 as against 104·5; t=6·18, p<·001).

During the time that random allocation was in operation, many changes occurred in the houses being compared and their significance for the research has been evaluated in the previous report (Clarke & Cornish, 1972). Two of the more important changes to affect the E House were (a) that the person who replaced the clinical psychologist as leader of the house in 1967 had more limited experience of group work†, and (b) that, owing to problems of over-crowding in the Third House, a number of attempts had to be made to broaden the basis of selection for the eligible group. It had originally been thought that boys considered eligible for random allocation would outnumber 'ineligibles' by a ratio of 2:1, since the regional classifying school made a practice of allocating those whom they considered to be the more disturbed and maladjusted boys to Kingswood Training School in preference to the other intermediate schools it served. The decision by the Home Office at the beginning of 1964 to base allocations to approved schools on geographical considerations in preference to allowing schools to admit particular types of boy regardless of where they lived, gradually forced the training school to admit a wider variety of boys than in previous years. This eventually resulted in the admission of larger numbers of duller boys and,

---

* A further result of such sharing was that some degree of 'contamination' between the two regimes may also have taken place. This is an objection which can be raised against other comparisons as well (Craft et al., 1964; Jesness, 1965) but the only recorded effects of contamination in the present research were to induce the C House, at certain points during the course of the trial, to try—unsuccessfully—to incorporate elements of the E House programme, such as group meetings, into its own regime.

† The change of housemaster in the C House during 1968 raised questions about *its* status as an adequate control.

as they were considered ineligible for the E House regime, the Third House soon became overcrowded.

Steps were taken by the Principal in 1966, in 1967, and again in 1968 to correct this imbalance by requesting E House staff to broaden the basis for admission,* but this created considerable resentment amongst E House staff who saw these moves as attempts to interfere with their own selection policy. As we have seen, however, analysis of data collected on the total sample of eligible boys, and on a smaller sample examined during a later period of the experiment, showed that IQ and Reading Age were always the most important variables determining selection throughout the course of the controlled trial. Analysis also showed that there was little difference in the subsequent 'success' of boys admitted to the E House earlier in the research as compared with those admitted later. Similarly, the effects of losing the clinical psychologist do not appear to have been as detrimental as it was imagined they would be at the time; the reconviction rates of those boys ($N=23$) who were in the House while he worked there were not significantly different from those admitted after he had left ($N=63$).

In the last resort, however, damage to the effectiveness of the E House by these or other problems experienced by staff (see Appendix 1) cannot be estimated on the basis of hindsight alone, since their primary impact was on the morale of those running the experimental programme. But teething troubles, compromises and confrontations are the lot of most new programmes which challenge traditional patterns of intervention and which create problems for an institution's existing administrative practices (Martin, 1962), and there is always the danger that giving details of these difficulties will, in the absence of comparable information from similar projects, tend to exaggerate the significance of problems which may, in fact, be no more than typical.† In practice, it was felt that the existence of the problems discussed in this section did not seriously affect the results of the controlled trial.

Adequacy of success criteria

Reconviction is sometimes criticised as a crude or insensitive criterion of the effectiveness of institutional programmes. Some of the force of this objection is lost when, as in the present research, a number of different methods were employed for measuring the extent and seriousness of further delinquency and how quickly it occurred. Other objections, such as the fact that our reconviction

---

* The Principal had consistently argued that, to be of any real value to the approved school service as a whole, the E House methods must—as well as being cost-effective—be applicable to a substantial proportion of approved school boys.
† Problems of securing adequate and uniform implementation of new methods, and of having to cope with unforeseen administrative difficulties, occur even in programmes planned with a degree of sophistication and a financial outlay which British research has not even begun to approach; Jesness et al.'s (1972) Youth Treatment Research Project devoted some 40,000 man-hours over five years to the training of staff at the two schools involved in that research.

data were not related to pre-programme delinquency, or that the data referred only to the official figures for crimes and did not take account of the larger number of crimes (the so-called 'dark figure') which are never detected, are of less importance when there is random allocation. Self-reported delinquency information was not in any case a feasible proposition for the present research.

Even when reconviction is accepted as the criterion, it is often argued that the follow-up period should be longer. It has been suggested that the evaluation of programme effectiveness is not possible until, for example, the subject marries or brings up children, presumably on the basis that the effects of a programme may be temporarily inhibited while re-integration into the home environment takes place. Quite apart from the fact that it could be argued equally well that any institutional programmes should temporarily inhibit an early return to crime, difficulties would arise in trying to ascribe longer-term effects unequivocally to 'causes' operating so long ago in the past. So many other events with claims to equal importance in influencing behaviour may have supervened and criminal activity, in any case, declines with advancing years. Common sense would expect the effects of institutional programmes to be limited and at their greatest when most recent. Leaving aside our own rather limited data (see page 17), other evidence from a longer term follow-up of ex-approved schoolboys (reported by Dr W H Hammond, formerly of the Home Office Research Unit, to a meeting of Approved School Psychologists at Sunningdale, 1968) and of US delinquents (McKay, 1967) indicate that longer periods provide an even gloomier picture of the proportion of releases who manage to avoid reconviction. Hammond's data—gathered on 254 senior approved schoolboys who passed through Redhill Classifying School during 1956 and who were followed up to their twenty-fifth birthdays—showed a reconviction rate of 73% for four years, and one of 79% for nine years. About 60% of his sample are described as having, by the end of the period, become continuous and persistent offenders, and about 40% of the total sample had received sentences of imprisonment as adults.

The relevance of reconviction

We have argued that of the various aims served by approved schools it is reasonable to give first place to rehabilitation as measured by reduction in post-institutional delinquency.

The Kingswood controlled trial, however, took place during the period when concepts of delinquency and appropriate intervention strategies were the subject of considerable public debate, which culminated in the passing of the Children and Young Persons Act 1969. Though reconviction was in the beginning considered by most people to constitute a relevant criterion, by the end of the research many working in the field had come to see delinquency more as a symptom of underlying problems of personal and social maladjustment, than as being of importance in its own right. Some other factors may also have contributed to the dissatisfaction with reconviction as a criterion; the gradual decline in approved school success rates* may have led to some loss of morale amongst the staff and a consequent disenchantment with a criterion which almost every year seemed to be setting a more severe standard by which their efforts were being judged. Furthermore, where staff are convinced that some of the things they are doing are producing visible changes in the attitudes and behaviour of their charges, they are tempted to assume that these changes will necessarily have an effect upon rehabilitation (See Appendix 3). If reconviction data do not bear out this belief, then the criterion understandably falls into disrepute amongst practitioners. Moreover, staff need both to evaluate their performance in the short-term and to utilize information gathered during a boy's stay in order to decide on matters such as the date of his discharge. Consequently, a number of 'intermediate' aims—such as changes in personality or attitudes—have come to be adopted, and these are served by corresponding 'intermediate' criteria. These often consist of the results of psychological tests or of informal estimates of attitudinal or behavioural change. Since staff have themselves to rely on such criteria, they may feel that their performance should be judged against these alone.†

Considerations such as these may also have been responsible for the more general confusion between methods and criteria which so often underlies discussions about reconviction data. Because traditional 'training' programmes, which emphasised the changing of behaviour, were commonly evaluated in terms of behavioural criteria such as reconviction, it somehow seemed inappropriate to use similar kinds of criteria for the evaluation of 'treatment' programmes which emphasised the changing of attitudes. It was as if, in other words, changes in methods justified or necessitated changes in aims and criteria. Given this position, reconviction data are seen as being at best ambiguous, and at worst, misleading. Evidence of behaviour change alone, such as the reduction of delinquency is, in the absence of evidence about intra-psychic changes, felt to be of questionable value because of the possibility that symptom-substitution may occur where the underlying 'disease' has not been treated. If, on the other hand, delinquent behaviour continues in the face of evidence of apparent changes in attitude, the behaviour may be dismissed on the grounds that, no longer fuelled by psychic conflict, it will eventually dwindle away.

There are, however, a number of practical objections to such viewpoints. Firstly, it is because of their delinquent behaviour and not their attitudes that children come to the attention of the authorities and are committed to residential

---

* Official figures show that of the boys released on after-care from the schools in 1954, 61% had not been reconvicted within three years after release; for boys released in 1967 this figure had dropped to 34% (HMSO, 1972). Some of the apparent drop in approved school success rates after 1956 can be attributed to improvement in procedures for obtaining data about reconvictions. On the other hand, the adoption of a standard list of offences, in 1963, restricted the collection of reconviction data on juveniles to these offences alone.

† There are few direct ways of measuring 'delinquency-proneness' during the boy's stay in the institution; although absconding might constitute a useful 'intermediate' criterion, many community homes no longer keep records of this behaviour.

programmes: there may well be many other unhappy, maladjusted and anti-authority children who are not delinquent and who therefore, do not find their way into the schools. Those actually running the institution are by no means the only, or even the most important, groups with an interest in deciding what the criteria for evaluating the effectiveness of such programmes should be. If it became known, not only that such institutions were relatively unsuccessful at reducing delinquency, but that they did not see themselves even as primarily concerned with changing this behaviour, it could become difficult to justify to the public either the existence of the institutions, or the removal of children from their homes.*

Secondly, it is not clear how staff wishing to improve long term personal adjustment—however defined—could achieve this without dealing with delinquency; for although it may not always be the case that an improvement in delinquent behaviour is accompanied by a corresponding improvement in attitudes, several investigations (Glueck & Glueck, 1934; Scott, 1964; Hood, 1966) indicate that post-programme recidivism is associated with continuing poor adjustment in many other areas of a person's life. The Gluecks comment:

> '... success or failure as measured by post-treatment recidivism is so highly reflective of success or failure in such other major fields of activity as industrial life, the meeting of family obligations, use of leisure, etc., that for practical purposes success or failure in respect of criminality may be used as a satisfactory index of success and failure in all major respects.'

Thus, although—according to psychodynamic theory—the possibility of symptom-substitution (in this case the substitution of other maladaptive behaviour for delinquency) can never be ruled out when the focus of intervention is solely or largely on changing the delinquent behaviour itself, whether such substitution does in fact occur is a matter for empirical investigation. Moreover, it should equally be recognised that therapeutic success cannot be claimed unless changes in behaviour, predicted as a result of apparent changes in personality or attitudes, actually take place.

Thirdly, to ignore reconviction information would mean having to rely on 'intermediate criteria' for the purposes of evaluation; but even those tests such as the Jesness Inventory which have been specially designed to measure reductions in delinquent attitudes as a result of intervention programmes perform rather poorly, and any measurable changes which occur seem unrelated to reconviction during the follow-up period (Mott, 1973). The absence of an association with reconviction renders many intermediate criteria such as these

---

* Logan (1972) comments that definitions of success: '... should be compatible with ordinary notions of what would be successful or unsuccessful outcomes of treatment. To be compatible with ordinary notions, "success" should refer to the correction or prevention of criminal behaviour, not to personal adjustment, happiness, mental health, employment, or family relations.'

of little use in determining whether the aim of reducing delinquency has been achieved.

Less extreme and more persuasive critics of reconviction suggest that institutional programmes should be regarded as only one component in the over-all intervention strategy. According to this view (Rapoport, 1960) there are two elements —treatment, or alteration of the personality towards better psychic integration, and rehabilitation, which consists of fitting the treated person back into the social environment from which he came. In the approved schools system these components are institutional intervention and after-care, respectively. On this analysis, two sets of success criteria are needed; one set (intermediate criteria) to measure the changes in personality and attitudes which have taken place as a result of institutional intervention, and another set (reconviction data) to measure the success of attempts to slot the individual back into society. While it is not denied that reconviction can be regarded as a satisfactory criterion by which the success of either the rehabilitation phase or the total intervention strategy can be evaluated, it is argued that reconviction data cannot be used to evaluate the institutional phase of the operation. High reconviction rates could, for example, be interpreted either as evidence that intervention had not been successful in the first place, or as evidence that any positive effects had been eroded as a result of poor after-care; intervention itself, so the argument would run, can only be evaluated by intermediate criteria. Though there is little evidence that current intermediate criteria measure delinquency-proneness satisfactorily, this fact alone cannot be used to discount the argument; if it were true, for example, that the Fricot Ranch Study's findings showed differential outcomes during at least part of the follow-up period,* this would seem to be some indication (assuming after-care conditions were similar for experimental and control groups) that the experimental programme had some effects, even though these were not picked up by the intermediate criteria used by Jesness. Results such as those of Scott (1964) showing an association between reconviction and evidence of continuing maladjustment can have no direct bearing on the successfulness of the residential programme phase of the total intervention process.

Although these arguments are characteristically used to defend 'treatment' programmes they are equally relevant to 'training' regimes, since both utilize a medical model of intervention which (as we shall argue in Chapter 6) overemphasises the contribution of personality and attitudes to delinquent behaviour and which, in consequence, tends to lay too much stress upon the importance of changing the individual. For the present, comment will be confined to questioning whether it is in practice worth while paying much attention to the

---

* As Jesness (1965) shows, random allocation was not able to prevent the presence of significant differences between the groups of boys admitted to the two programmes; these differences raise the question of whether differential outcomes occurred solely as a result of different programmes.

relative abilities of different methods used during the institutional phase of the total intervention process to produce changes in the individual delinquent when:

a. there is little evidence that they occur;
b. if they occur they are difficult to measure directly by means of existing intermediate criteria;
c. if occurring, and measurable by intermediate criteria, they are not usually correlated with reconviction;
d. if occurring, whether measurable or not, and if associated with reconviction, their effects dissipate so rapidly.

In this chapter it has been argued that the results of the Kingswood controlled trial which showed no differences in the success rates of 'training' and 'treatment' regimes* could not be accounted for by inadequate implementation of therapeutic community principles or by limitations in the criterion of effectiveness employed. Negative findings such as these nevertheless usually lead to calls for better implementation of programme principles and to demands for more rigorous evaluative designs to enable even finer discriminations between programme outcomes to be drawn. Criticisms of much existing evaluative research are no doubt justified (see Logan, 1972†), but the proponents of institutional intervention seem to be in some danger of using these objections as a way of dismissing the body of uncomfortable evidence that has been accumulating from a large number of studies.

---

* These terms were defined on page two of Chapter 1.
† Logan, however, also points out that there is some evidence that the sounder the research design, the less likely it is that differential outcomes will be reported.

CHAPTER 5

The Results of Previous Evaluative Research

Differential effectiveness of approved school regimes

Apart from the fact that the E and C House success rates did not differ, perhaps the most important finding of the present research was that those for the Third House were not significantly different from those of the other two houses—despite the fact that its programme was much less clearly defined and that staffing difficulties had contributed to its unsettled state throughout the course of the research. The question was therefore raised, in a very direct way, as to whether the content of institutional programmes, given similar intakes,* makes much difference to the behaviour of their inmates after release. Even greater point was given to this question by the fact that the success rates of therapeutic communities operating in two other approved schools in the region were found not to differ significantly from those of the three houses at Kingswood (see Chapter 4). These findings are consistent with previous research by McMichael (1974), who found no significant differences when she compared the reconviction rates of boys released from Loaningdale (a Scottish approved school run as a kind of therapeutic community) with those of a control group from other schools, and by Craft (1965), who found that an exceptionally well-organised 'family-type' programme in one junior approved school failed to produce better than average results. Together, all these results suggest that differences in programmes, whether in theoretical principles (as was the case at Kingswood) or in modes of implementation (as was the case with the various kinds of therapeutic communities both in England and Scotland) fail to produce differences in outcome for the approved school population.

Certain differences in reconviction rates have been observed amongst English approved schools, however, and these might on the basis of recent research be at least partially explained by the operation—planned or unplanned—of factors in the school environment. Sinclair & Clarke (1973), for example, found that the reconviction rates of 66 approved schools were significantly associated with schools' absconding rates, even when differences amongst intakes to the schools had been allowed for. Dunlop (1975) found that although differences in intake to the eight schools she studied played a very large part in determining relative success rates at the end of a five year follow-up period, certain salient features of school regimes (as perceived by her respondents) also appeared to make a small contribution towards these differences; one of her results indicated that schools which emphasised trade training and responsible behaviour in the school had lower absconding and higher success rates than other schools.

---

* Intake to the Third House was not significantly worse than to the other two houses in terms of variables (such as previous delinquent history) found to be associated with extent of future delinquency.

Despite the numbers of boys and institutions involved in both studies, these effects were small.* Their results do, however, provide some evidence against the suggestion that nothing that institutional programmes do, or omit to do, makes any difference to the likelihood of subsequent delinquent behaviour by their inmates. But they still fail to offer satisfactory support for the view that some programmes are more effective at *reducing* delinquency than others. It may rather be that programmes described as 'better' are those whose effects are neutral rather than beneficial while in comparison those described as 'worse' actually increase the chances of a boy's behaving in a delinquent manner after he is released from the institutional programme. We will return to this point later in the chapter.

Other findings concerning differential effectiveness

A pattern of predominantly negative findings is revealed in the reviews by Bailey (1966), Morris (1971), Robison and Smith (1971), and Martinson (1974) of a large amount of mainly American evaluative research into the differential effectiveness of institutional intervention. Differential outcomes have not emerged from the important studies of the last few years which have dealt with juvenile delinquents and which have utilized some method of satisfactorily matching inputs to the programmes being compared (eg Jesness, 1971; Empey & Lubeck, 1971; Jesness et al., 1972). In those cases (eg the original Highfields research of Weeks, 1958, and Jesness's Fricot Ranch Study, 1965) where differences in outcomes were found, there may be considerable doubt about the validity of the results because of breakdowns in, or lack of, adequate input matching. The results from studies of older offenders in this country follow a similar pattern: Craft et al.'s (1964) controlled trial of authoritarian and permissive intervention programmes for adolescent psychopaths found no differences between the two regimes in numbers of boys subsequently offending, while Bottoms & McClintock (1974) found that two different borstal regimes—one giving traditional, the other more individualised, training—produced similar post-institutional reconviction rates.

Again, however, there are studies which appear to run counter to the general trend of evaluative research in this area. Four studies in particular—two with adult prisoners (Berntsen & Christiansen, 1965; Shaw, 1974), and two with older juvenile offenders (Adams, 1961; Williams, 1970) may be regarded as evidence against the view that the content of institutional programmes has little or no effect on reconviction rates, and because of this some discussion of their findings is necessary.

In Berntsen & Christiansen's research a sample of short-term prisoners was chosen at random from the prison population of Copenhagen† to participate in

---

* In the Kingswood controlled trial research no relation was found between absconding and the likelihood of subsequent reconviction—a further indication that such relationships are rather weak.

† It is not clear whether all prisoners in the study's sample attended the same prison. If they did not, this raises further problems for the interpretation of the study's findings.

a resocialisation project. This experimental group was offered some degree of individual therapy in combination with welfare measures—assistance in finding a job and accommodation on release, help in sorting out family problems, etc.— during their term of imprisonment. A control group, consisting of those with prison numbers nearest to those of the E group, received only normal social work contact. Results were claimed to indicate that the experimental intervention programme significantly reduced recidivism rates. These findings must, however, be treated with some caution; the authors' definition of recidivism is based on information about the nature of sentences imposed by the courts on reconvicted offenders in the E and C groups. Moreover, the categories 'no subsequent convictions' and 'fines/simple detention' are defined as 'non-recidivist' for the analysis of follow-up data. It was pointed out in Chapter 3 that the use of court disposals as a basis for measuring extent of post-intervention delinquency may be less accurate than independent ratings of offence-seriousness or, more simply, reconviction rates alone. Courts' decisions may be influenced by factors such as the offender's previous criminal history or, more seriously, by knowledge of the offender's status as an experimental or control subject— particularly if after-care agencies are themselves aware of this. When Berntsen and Christiansen's data are recalculated, using reconviction as the criterion, no significant differences emerge; even when the authors' criterion is used, but taking account of the significantly larger numbers of 'chronic criminals' in the C group, no significant differences are to be found.

The results of a more specific form of intervention were reported by Shaw (1974) whose research studied the effects of extended contact with a caseworker on reconviction rates of prisoners in two prisons—one, an 'open' prison, the other a 'closed' one. From the populations of each prison a sample of men were chosen at random; these were then allocated at random within each prison to experimental and control groups. When the number reconvicted from the total experimental group (regardless of which prison they came from) was compared with the number reconvicted from the total control group at the end of the follow-up period it was found that significantly fewer of the experimental group had been reconvicted.

Since the report indicates the existence of substantial differences between the regimes, populations and organisation of social work in the two prisons, it may be considered preferable to treat the results from each separately. When this is done, a more conservative estimate of the degree of association between extended social work contact and reconviction emerges: results for the open prison fail to show significant differences between its E and C groups, while for the closed prison the association, though significant, is considerably reduced.

Of the two studies of older juvenile offenders, Williams' study of three open borstals which ran, respectively, 'casework', 'group-counselling' and 'traditional' regimes, found the 'casework' regime to be significantly more successful than the others, but this may well have been because of the significantly larger numbers of inmates who were apparently transferred out of this programme. As the overall reconviction rate for transferred youths in the total sample was very much higher (78%) than for those who completed their stay (59%) it is probable that evidence of differential effectiveness would disappear if reconviction rates were calculated on the basis of those admitted rather than on those who completed their stay (see Chapter 3's discussion of 'culling').

Lastly, the Pilot Intensive Counselling Organisation (PICO) Project (Adams, 1961) studied the effect of individual interview therapy on two groups of older delinquents at the Deuel Vocational Institution. One group was characterised as 'amenable' to the experimental programme, the other group as 'non-amenable', and youths from each group were allocated at random to experimental and control groups. For the non-amenable group, follow-up information provided no evidence of differences in subsequent delinquent behaviour between the E and C groups. For the amenables, the E group was found to be significantly superior to the C group on a number of follow-up measures. When E and C amenables were compared on a number of characteristics previously found to be relevant to post-institutional failure, the latter group was found to be somewhat worse; Adams concludes, however, that the differences (which were not significant) had no effect on the research findings as a whole. A more serious question is raised by the lack of relatively objective success criteria such as arrest rates or reconviction rates for the E and C groups. Instead, measures were used such as parole revocation, unfavourable discharge, or months of return to state custody (decisions concerning which may more easily be influenced by parole agent's or court's knowledge of an individual's status as an E or C subject).*

These studies have been discussed at some length because more importance is often accorded to the small numbers of studies which appear to reject the null hypothesis (no differences between treatments) than to the considerable numbers of other studies which have repeatedly failed to do so. For the present it would be unsafe to place too much emphasis upon their results, until they can be confirmed by further research which takes into consideration the criticisms outlined.

Because there has been a dearth of evidence to support the contention that institutional programmes may be differentially effective in reducing delinquency, it is often argued that similar success rates for different institutional programmes dealing with similar populations conceal interactions between the programmes and sub-groups of the total populations allocated to them. Attempts have been made to develop offender typologies and classifications with a view to comparing the success rates of different programmes for various homogeneous sub-groups of delinquent populations. Results to date, however, have failed to produce

---

* Knowledge of an offender's previous status by after-care agents may, of course, effect even reconviction rates if the agent is thereby encouraged to pay special attention to E group members during the follow-up period.

statistically satisfactory evidence* of offender-programme interactions (Jesness, 1971; Jesness et al., 1972) despite increasingly sophisticated developments in both typologies and intervention programmes.

The overall effectiveness of institutional programmes

If, as has been argued, it is type of intake which primarily determines outcomes† this does not, of itself, deny that institutions may have an effect on subsequent offending, but implies only that their influence may be a relatively constant one regardless of identifiable differences in programmes. The question would, of course, still remain as to whether in general this constant influence operated in a positive, neutral or negative way on the rate of subsequent offending.

The question of the success of institutional programmes in absolute terms, although of considerable public interest, appears to have been raised comparatively rarely in institutional research, which has been primarily occupied in ascertaining how such programmes—assumed a priori to be beneficial—could be improved. The actual success rates of approved schools offer little ground for optimism. While the rates for individual schools differ considerably, such variations have been largely attributed to differences in intake (Dunlop, 1975), and overall success rates for a three-year period are only of the order of 30%–35% (HMSO, 1972). Moreover, though even this figure is often put forward as evidence of the schools' effectiveness, such estimations of 'success' rely on the improbable assumption that *all* boys admitted to approved schools would have remained, or become more, delinquent had they been left at home.

There are a number of reasons for regarding this assumption as an unlikely one. Firstly, schools often claim that varying proportions of their admission are not delinquent at all (though most, in fact, have been found guilty by the courts at some time in the past). Just as it would be disingenuous to claim these cases as 'successes' merely on the grounds that they continued to stay out of trouble, so—should they become delinquent following their stay in an approved school—they must be regarded as something more serious than simply 'failures'. Secondly, it is probable that because of the combined effects of maturation, spontaneous remission, and statistical regression a further sizeable proportion of the intake would, regardless of the influence of particular programmes—or, indeed, of whether they were sent to an institution or not—be less likely to

---

* As Bottoms & McClintock (1968) point out, where a population is divided into 'types', without reference to important background factors which influence prior probabilities of reconviction, and the total population of which they form sub-groups is randomly allocated to different programmes, there is no reason to suppose that this design will ensure that similar sub-groups—one entering an experimental programme and one entering a control programme—will be equivalent with respect to risk of failure. In such cases, results purporting to demonstrate offender-programme interactions may once more show that these differences occurred merely because of differences in the criminality of intakes to the two programmes.

† It is assumed, of course, that the post-institutional environment is similar for the populations being compared.

offend subsequently. Thirdly, it will be shown later that non-institutional intervention strategies may often be equally as effective in containing subsequent offending as institutional programmes. When qualified in this way, success rates of the order of 30% for those admitted to approved schools look decidedly unsatisfactory, especially when it is remembered that the reconvictions upon which these rates are based occur during the after-care supervision period, and that reconviction data collected over longer-term periods show even lower success-rates. Developments in techniques of assessment and allocation to different types of schools, the increased numbers of professional and trained staff, and the use of a more psychological and humanitarian approach have not been successful in raising the low success rates of the schools. The extent of the failure of institutional intervention to justify itself was succinctly described by Healy & Bronner as long ago as 1928:

> 'If . . . it is insisted that the many failures among those committed simply means that the worst offenders are the committed, we may offer the argument that, even so, the correctional institution is masquerading falsely if it fails to correct large percentages. It is as if one argued that some hospital showed very poor results in cures because all the people who went there were sick people. . . . Failures in any event certainly bespeak ineffectiveness of treatment. Delinquents are sent to institutions to be cured'.

If, as has been argued, absolute success-rates are so low, a tentative answer may now be given to the question posed at the beginning of this section—whether institutional programmes have a positive, neutral, or negative influence upon the rate of subsequent offending. From the evidence so far presented it seems likely that, as mentioned earlier, institutional programmes described as 'better' are those which perform a largely holding operation in relation to delinquent behaviour—neither increasing nor reducing its likelihood in the post-institutional environment to any appreciable extent.

Sinclair & Clarke's and Dunlop's research findings may enable us to take the argument a little further, since they and some of the other research we have discussed appear to show some small degree of association between reconviction rates and factors in the institutional programme. It is particularly the case with the approved school research, however, that differences in success rates amongst schools are more readily explicable in terms of the omissions of the less successful programmes than the effectiveness of the more successful. Schools which permit absconding, for example, may by so doing be providing further opportunities for boys to engage in delinquent behaviour while at school; those schools, on the other hand, which emphasise current control of delinquency by reducing opportunities for absconding may at least avoid providing boys with new delinquent learning experiences.* If this is so, it may be concluded that it is

---

* Even with the relatively small sample of the Kingswood research, it was found that boys who had been found guilty of committing offences during their stay were significantly more likely to be reconvicted afterwards (see Appendix II).

more accurate to talk of the harmful effects of some programmes than to extol the virtues of others, whose main value may be that they avoid the potentially damaging effects of institutional life.

Institutional versus non-institutional intervention

It is often maintained that it is impossible to establish the effectiveness of residential intervention in absolute terms unless its outcome is compared with that of a 'no-treatment' control group. In practice, these objections have little force when success rates of the low levels so far discussed are concerned. Residential programmes can, however, be compared with other modes of intervention, and such comparisons can provide further evidence bearing on the effectiveness of institution-based programmes. In research reported in 'The Sentence of the Court' (Home Office, 1969), offenders aged under 17 who received different kinds of disposal were followed up for a five-year period. Expected reconviction rates were calculated on the basis of information relating to the offender's age, number of court appearances (or offences taken into consideration) and type of offence—factors found to be associated with the likelihood of reconviction. The relevant figures are reproduced below; scores over 100 imply that the measure has a worse reconviction rate than expected, while those below 100 are better than expected:

	1st Offenders	*Offenders with previous convictions*
Discharge	89	100
Fine	75	83
Probation	118	101
Approved School	138	102

These results must be treated with some caution; samples involved were, in some cases, small and, discussing the bases upon which expected rates of future offending were calculated, the author comments that: 'The courts may have made allowance for factors not recorded in the documents available for research, and the possibility cannot be ignored that particular sentences may have been used more frequently for the "worse" or for the "better" offenders in any of the categories studied'. Very few first offenders, for example, are sentenced to institutional programmes so that to some extent they constitute a special group whose committal may have been influenced by factors, such as poor home backgrounds, which made their prognoses worse than those for the usual run of first offenders. Despite this, the fact remains that first offenders sent to approved schools did considerably worse in terms of reconviction than those disposed of by the courts in other ways, while even for recidivists other measures appeared to be as, or more, effective. Indeed, it was disposals such as discharge or fining which involved least direct intervention in the daily lives of the offenders which appeared to achieve the more satisfactory results.

Similar conclusions are reached by Harlow (1970) and Martinson (1974) who, in their surveys of research comparing the effectiveness of intensive intervention

THE RESULTS OF PREVIOUS EVALUATIVE RESEARCH

within the community with that of institutional programmes, found the former to be no less effective than the latter, when dealing with similar intakes. While evaluation of community-based programmes is still not sufficiently rigorous* (and while it is clearly inappropriate for the minority of dangerous offenders) Harlow comments that on the available evidence ' . . . it is appropriate to suggest that less costly, less personally damaging alternatives be utilized wherever they are at least as effective as imprisonment . . .'. Such conclusions clearly have relevance to the use of institutional intervention for younger offenders.

But it is doubtful whether the wholesale substitution of non-institutional programmes for institutional ones would appreciably improve the post-programme reconviction rates of their participants; just as the low absolute success rates of institutional programmes raise questions about the relevance of their methods and the theoretical basis from which these are developed, so the similarly low success rates of non-institutional programmes raise questions about their viability as solutions to the problem of reducing delinquent behaviour. In the next chapter an attempt will be made to discover why neither approach as currently practised has proved very satisfactory.

---

* Studies frequently neglect, for instance, to specify the offending-rate during the course of a community-based programme.

CHAPTER 6

Explaining the Ineffectiveness of Residential Intervention

The previous five chapters have argued that residential programmes are largely ineffective in reducing the incidence of subsequent delinquent behaviour. It is of little value, however, to say that something does not work unless one can explain why. In this chapter an attempt is made to provide such an explanation, albeit of a tentative and sketchy nature, for the failure of institutional intervention.

The traditional model of intervention

Current institutional programmes, whether 'treatment' or 'training', rely on a 'disease' model of delinquency and a 'medical' model of intervention. According to these, since the main source of behavioural variance lies within the individual the primary focus of therapy should be on changing the individual. More specifically, the residential programme is seen to serve a similar function with regard to delinquency to that of the hospital in the treatment of physical or mental diseases; thus the individual is temporarily removed from an environment which either actively maintains his 'disease' or within which therapeutic measures cannot be satisfactorily organised. In the 'hospital' are provided both a temporary isolation from disease-provoking stimuli and, perhaps, more positive treatment facilities through which the 'disease' itself can be cured, and subsequent attacks prevented by the building up of an individual's resistance.

Both 'treatment' and 'training' operate according to this model, and both emphasise the importance of creating changes within the individual whilst he is inhabiting a milieu which is optimally organised to permit and further behavioural change. Although sharing the same basic intervention model, however, these approaches differ considerably over the way in which such behaviour change can be achieved. At the risk of creating artificial distinctions in an area where eclecticism and semantic confusion already make description of differences between methods difficult, it seems to us that 'treatment' approaches characteristically emphasise the importance of dealing with individual maladjustment since, it is claimed, it is this which predisposes the offender towards delinquent behaviour. The maladjustment is seen to arise from faults in the socialisation and educational processes which create and maintain anti-social attitudes or deviant personality. Delinquent behaviour is regarded as a sign, or an 'acting out', of these psychological problems, and can be reduced only as a result of their resolution. Although some role is given to the individual's current environment in maintaining delinquent behaviour, it is stressed that this is primarily internally-motivated. It is for this reason that it is believed that delinquent, or functionally equivalent, behaviour will continue to occur so long as the sources of the maladjustment are not sought out and removed. 'Treatment' is therefore mainly concerned with changing attitudes and looks to changes in behaviour only as a consequence of improvements in personal adjustment.

'Training' approaches—and we include under this general category both the more traditional type of approved school methods and those run on behaviour modification principles—are more concerned with the changing of behaviour, by means of programmes which develop pro-social responses through appropriate rewards and punishments. The methods are characteristically less concerned with psychotherapeutic techniques and individual casework to develop 'insight' and hence bring about cognitive and attitudinal changes, and more with the direct manipulation of behaviour—though it is hoped that the bringing about of changes in behaviour, together with the improvements in inter-personal relationships which can come from communal living and from practical counselling, will eventually lead to changes in attitudes. Here, as in 'treatment' approaches, it is the individual's internal motivation which is ultimately seen as the primary source of behavioural variance.

One explanation for the failure of current institutional programmes which is sometimes put forward is that we are often too optimistic about the extent of human malleability, particularly that of adolescents. As Roberts et al. (1974) argue in connection with their evaluation of the effectiveness of 'outward-bound' types of training schemes, it may be a mistake—and part of a general myth about the nature of adolescence—to believe that short institutional programmes can effect significant changes in the attitudes or behaviour of young people, where such expectations would not be held for adults.* They conclude that '... whatever psychological changes are effected by the schemes are insufficiently strong to change the course of young peoples' lives once they have returned to their usual environments'. This interpretation of the findings, however, suggests that more intensive schemes might bring about more powerful psychological changes which would in turn be sufficiently strong to have a permanent effect. This, however, merely leads to conventional demands for more and 'better' forms of institutional intervention along similar lines even though quite intensive and lengthy programmes dealing with young (and therefore presumably the more malleable) delinquents have failed in the past to provide satisfactory evidence of effectiveness.

Though the evidence so far presented could be construed as showing that personality and attitudes (and hence behaviour) are resistant to manipulation, it is a matter of everyday experience that human behaviour can change.

---

* The following passage nicely summarises their views:

> 'Neither sponsors nor course organisers intimate as a body that adults, whose leisure revolves around the pub or bingo hall, could be rescued from these "temptations" by a four-week course. Nor is a period in the countryside generally regarded as a feasible strategy for increasing the productivity of adult workers or dealing with truculent shop stewards. But young people are considered to be different. More profitable uses of leisure, responsiveness in the work situation and attitudes towards those in authority are considered susceptible to short periods of treatment operating upon adolescents' characters.'

Moreover, one need not deny the experience of practitioners that attitude and behaviour changes occur within residential programmes, nor that different programmes may elicit contrasting behaviours from their inmates. Indeed, the institutional setting, with its restricted opportunities for delinquent behaviour, and its powers of surveillance and control which enable behaviour to be more certainly punished or rewarded than is possible elsewhere, can impose conformity and reduce misbehaviour. Thus when considering the effectiveness of institutional programmes, the salient fact is not that changes of attitude or modification of behaviour do not occur, but that for the most part the gains made do not appear to carry over into the post-institutional environment (Sinclair, 1971).

This failure to consolidate gains made during institutional intervention is as much a feature of 'training' as of 'treatment' programmes. In token economies, for example, where therapy is directed primarily towards bringing about changes in behaviour, the problems of generalising behaviour gains to the post-institutional environment, or of resisting their extinction there, have yet to be given adequate consideration (Kazdin & Bootzin, 1972). Where programmes stress the importance of manipulating the inmate's environment through the systematic application of operant and classical conditioning procedures (Haley, 1974), it is the institutional environment's very capacity to exert far-reaching control over rewards and punishments for the purpose of promoting pro-social behaviour which distinguishes it from the post-institutional situation.

The difficulty of transferring behaviour learned in one setting to another one may explain the failure of both 'treatment' and 'training' approaches. In the former case the lack of transfer may simply be due to the fact that behaviour is determined less by highly generalised response predispositions such as attitudes or personality traits than by the particular setting in which it occurs. Moreover, if this is the case it might also explain the poor results of 'training' programmes, since one would only expect behaviours exhibited or changed in one environment to be maintained in another where the two environments shared important characteristics in common.*

Yet, although current intervention programmes may pay lip service to the influence of the offender's immediate environment as one of the determinants of his behaviour, and not withstanding the direct evidence that the different institutional environments offered by approved schools can themselves selectively elicit or inhibit certain behaviours in the institution regardless of personality or other intake factors (see Clarke & Martin's (1971) research on absconding), the schools (now community homes) continue to base their programmes upon a view of the genesis and regulation of delinquent behaviour which fails to take

---

* In the Fricot Ranch Study (Jesness, 1965) it was found that no correlation existed either between numbers of incident reports (records of infractions of institutional rules) and parole violation, or between lodge grade (based upon good behaviour) and success on parole. It is not always clear, however, to what extent findings such as these reflect differences in environments (stimulus generalisation) or differences between behaviours (response generalisation).

adequate account of the importance of the offender's immediate environment as a continuous influence upon his behaviour, before, during and after institutional intervention.

An alternative model of intervention

Perhaps the most pervasive influence upon practice in institutional intervention has been that of personality psychology, which emphasises the importance of enduring personal predispositions in eliciting and regulating behaviour. In his re-appraisal of the results of traditional personality research Mischel (1968) attacks the belief that an individual's behaviour can be explained largely in terms of his personal characteristics and with little reference to his immediate situation. As he points out, if they were of paramount importance, enduring personality traits and states should ensure that behaviour is consistent across situations and stable over time, but the research reviewed by Mischel provides evidence of only low (though statistically significant) coefficients of situational consistency and temporal stability. These correlations, since they can account for only a very small proportion of behavioural variance, argue for the relative unimportance of broad personality traits.* He concludes that:

'... with the possible exception of intelligence, highly generalised behavioural consistencies have not been demonstrated and the concept of personality traits as broad response predispositions is thus untenable'.

The social learning theory of behaviour which Mischel offers as an alternative to traditional personality theory looks for the determinants of behaviour in the environmental conditions which co-vary with its occurrence, maintenance and change. The theory seeks order and regularity, not in the shape of consistency of behaviour *across* situations, but in the form of general propositions which relate environmental changes to behaviour changes. In attempting to show how experience regulates and changes behaviour, Mischel indicates the ways in which a social learning theory can produce an account of behaviour which is consistent with its specificity; *behaviour is seen to depend on the exact stimulus conditions in the evoking situation and on an individual's previous experience of similar situations.* This model of behaviour implies that intervention should aim to modify the consequences of behaviour (its reinforcements) and the emotion-arousing properties of stimuli rather than to attempt to bring about some more fundamental change in the responding individual himself.

---

* As Mischel (1973a) comments, psychodynamic theory, while also postulating the existence of stable, relatively general underlying motivational dispositions, allows that overt behaviour is not highly consistent, but accounts for this by recognising the influence of the behaviour setting in determining the *form* which the behaviour will take. In this way, diverse (but allegedly functionally-equivalent) behaviours may be claimed to serve the same underlying dispositions or complexes. Such a view is more difficult to challenge except (a) by testing the effectiveness of intervention strategies based upon the theory and (b) by empirically testing its corollaries—such as the prediction that symptom-substitution will occur, where only the overt behaviour and not the underlying psychological processes are changed.

Before exploring further the consequences of this account of behaviour, one important objection must be countered. In the previous chapter it was argued that factors concerning various aspects of an individual's previous offence history can be used to calculate expected rates of future offending. It might therefore be held that these factors are akin to the very response predispositions or personality traits—in this case 'criminality'—to which Mischel takes exception. But although the fact that one can apparently predict an individual's future responses on the basis of past ones may seem to argue against the view that the current environment is an important determinant of behaviour, there is a crucial difference between the role played by past experience in affecting future behaviour, and the role ascribed to personality traits. Past experience, rather than creating in the individual stable and consistent personality traits, equips him instead *with an ever-expanding set of potential behavioural responses;* but these behaviours, since they were originally elicited in particular situations, will only be repeated when the latter recur. Thus the persistence in the criminal behaviour of certain individuals, despite the treatment they are given and the measures taken against them, may largely be accounted for by the fact that there is little change in the environments which they normally inhabit.

In everyday speech we tend to neglect to specify the environment, except by implication; in part this is because we tend to encounter people in a restricted range of behaviour settings and to limit our predictions about their behaviour to these environments alone. Under such stable circumstances the relationship between behaviour and environment, though still important, is often relatively constant and does not have to be taken into account when making predictions about behaviour; it is because of this that dispositional labels such as personality traits have come to be seen as assuming a greater role in determining behaviour than would be warranted if there were a careful and explicit specification of the environment.* It is only when an individual's behavioural responses are examined in relation to a wider variety of settings than those in which we normally encounter them that the crucial role of the environment becomes apparent. As Barker (1968) comments:

> 'When . . . we made long records of children's behaviour in real-life settings in accordance with a traditional person-centred approach, we found that some attributes of behaviour varied less across children within settings than across settings within the days of children. We found, in short, that we could predict some aspects of children's behaviour more adequately from knowledge of the behaviour characteristics of the drugstores, arithmetic classes, and

---

* A discussion of the extent to which trait labels (extraversion, neuroticism, anxiety etc) can have useful classificatory and predictive functions is beyond the scope of this paper. Even commonly-used trait labels, such as honesty, which appear to define a relatively restricted set of behaviours, may be less consistent across situations than is customarily thought (Hartshorne & May, 1928). Intimate knowledge of a person's behaviours, and of the wide variety of settings in which these behaviours occur, may enable one to apply such trait labels usefully for descriptive and predictive purposes; those used in traditional personality theory, however, tend to be rather less precise.

basketball games they inhabited than from knowledge of the behaviour tendencies of particular children . . .'

In the course of this discussion we have laid particular stress upon the contribution of the environment to behaviour and, in recognition of this emphasis, prefer to use the term 'environmental/learning theory' to express the salient feature of this approach rather than the more general term, 'social learning theory'.

One way of expressing the difference between the viewpoints of environmental/learning theory and those of traditional personality theory is illustrated by the following example: when an individual is placed in a situation where a delinquent response is possible—for example, taking a car without the owner's consent—he may engage in the delinquent behaviour for a number of reasons; he may be bored; he may want to go somewhere in a hurry; it may be raining, late at night, or in a place where public transport is not available; he may have been drinking and he may be encouraged to take the car by companions. The behaviour initially occurs, then, as a result of a chance motivational state rather than an enduring personal predisposition, in combination with environmental opportunities which offer possible responses as a solution.

Once made, however, this response takes up a permanent place in that individual's behavioural repertoire, its position in the response hierarchy being governed by the various reinforcements which accompanied its original performance. Thus it becomes a part of that past experience which he brings to any new situation, and in this sense it has some affinities with traditional concepts about predispositions. The important differences are that the response is a specific behaviour (not all delinquent activities, but only car-stealing)*, and that whether he makes the same response again will depend, firstly, on whether he subsequently finds himself in a situation similar to the original setting in which the delinquent behaviour took place, and, secondly, on the extent to which the response was previously reinforced in that setting. Possessing the response does not of itself predispose him to use it, although experiencing reinforcement of a particular behaviour in a certain behaviour setting may encourage an individual actively to seek out such settings in the future in order to perform the behaviour, regardless of the reasons which led him to do so in the first place.

Although some early experimentation has given grounds for criticism (cf. Mischel, 1973a), it should be stressed that an environmental/learning theory approach to the task either of explaining or of modifying behaviour is neither necessarily naive nor anti-individualistic. Indeed, since—as both Mischel and Cliffe et al. (1974) comment—the approach calls for detailed analysis of the behaviour patterns of individuals, it is necessary to tailor intervention strategies to individual needs in a much more systematic and rigorous way than institutional programmes currently achieve. Nor, as Bandura (1974) and Mischel

---

* A particular individual may, of course, depending on the environment he inhabits, separately acquire a wide range of delinquent behaviours.

(1973b) discuss at length, does an essentially behaviourist approach necessarily imply a crude determinism. While opinions differ as to the contribution made by persons and situations to behavioural variance (Golding, 1975), emphasis upon the importance of the effects of different environmental arrangements does not of itself deny the place that individual differences (in terms, for example, of past learning) may have in the expression of particular behaviours, especially in interaction with environmental conditions. Rather does it stress that it is of practical importance to recognise that substantial proportions of the variance in behaviour are accounted for by situational variables, including, of course, other people (Moos, 1973). The theory therefore demands some change of therapeutic emphasis; as Moos (1974) comments:

> 'Our central tasks of understanding, predicting, and changing behaviour compel us to learn more about environmental dimensions and to formulate valid concepts about them. The optimal arrangement of environments is probably the most powerful behaviour modification technique we currently have available.'

Implications of the alternative model

The placing of greater emphasis upon the environmental determinants of behaviour has important consequences for institutional intervention, since it indicates that their stress upon 'boy-changing', which has led them to try to treat the individual in isolation from his characteristic environment, has been to some extent misplaced. For while removal to an institution may protect a child temporarily from the environments which elicited and maintained his delinquent responses, attempting to change behaviour in one setting by working upon it in another does nothing—of itself—to alter the original environmental factors and, in consequence, the probability that delinquent behaviour patterns will be resurrected when the offender has completed the institutional programme. While in theory the intervention environment could be made more like the natural one, it is unfortunately the case that the more therapeutically useful the institutional environment is designed to be, the less it approximates to the real world outside, and the less likelihood, therefore, there is for behaviour to generalise.

Moreover, institutional programmes often have—for one reason or another—to ignore important sources of reinforcement in the offender's own environment (some of which may work against therapy), simply because these are not capable of being utilized by the programme. Lastly, institutional settings provide fewer opportunities for manifestation of delinquent behaviour and, in consequence, there are few occasions when it is possible to attempt direct modification of the behaviour by manipulation of reinforcement contingencies. Such delinquency as does take place occurs characteristically, not within the institution but—following absconding and during leave—in the outside community. This means that it is regulated by variables over which the institution can have little control or influence.

Although the environmental/learning model of behaviour explains why institutional programmes are inappropriate instruments of behaviour change, the alternatives it advocates provide no ready panacea. In the first place it should be recognized that current forms of non-institutional treatment for delinquents, such as probation or community service, would receive no more support under the model; for these too tend to proceed by seeking to bring about change in the offender rather than his environment. In the second place, as McKissack (1967) points out, it is difficult to secure changes in the environment that are likely to alter substantially the life pattern of an individual. The environmental/learning theory approach to delinquency is therefore somewhat less optimistic than traditional personality theory about the possibility of making once-and-for-all changes in human behaviour. For if performing a new act permanently expands an individual's behavioural repertoire, then subsequent intervention must remain content with utilizing social control mechanisms to reduce the extent to which this potential response is entertained when similar circumstances arise in the future. These mechanisms are of three types, and involve the reduction of opportunities to commit delinquent acts, the use of behaviour modification techniques, or those of 'reality therapy'.

Since it is an individual's environment which provides him with opportunities for delinquent behaviour, it would seem that such activities could be made more difficult to carry out simply by making selective changes, either to the individual's own personal environment, or to the social environment in general. One practical example of the latter is the fitting of steering-column locks to all cars sold in this country since 1971. An important characteristic of this type of approach is that the changes to be made are clearly-defined and limited in scope, and relate directly to the setting in which particular types of delinquent acts take place, with the intention of thereby reducing the likelihood of their occurrence. These changes, which may be particularly appropriate to certain types of casual offending, are to be distinguished from more general social crime prevention policies such as alleviating poverty, or improving housing or education.

Alternatively, it may be possible to prevent the individual's gaining access to those settings which, in the past, have been the scene of his delinquent activities. This sort of restriction—whether of hooligans from football grounds, or child-molesters from places where they are most likely to meet potential victims—has the advantage over traditional custodial measures that direct control is exerted over those environmental factors alone which elicit and maintain the prohibited behaviour, without the grosser interference and possibly harmful effects of institutional intervention. It may also cause less inconvenience to law-abiding citizens than the sorts of blanket restrictions on behaviour which are apt to be created by changes to the environment less specifically related to particular individuals. Its disadvantages are that it may involve a considerable amount of surveillance work—either of the individual or of the setting—and that it is often difficult to specify the relevant behaviour settings with sufficient clarity. Much more research into the latter is required, although pioneer work in behaviour setting theory has already been carried out by Barker (1968) and his associates, while Moos (1973) has reviewed some of the wide range of research on human environments.

Unlike the foregoing methods, the second main approach involves direct manipulation of a person's behaviour by changing the likelihood of its being performed. In this case, behaviour modification techniques based on learning theory can be used to manipulate the reinforcements which follow the forbidden activity in order to reduce its status in the individual's response hierarchy. Thus, while it may always remain available as a potential response every time the individual is placed in an environment similar to that in which the original response was made, it will gradually come to be less strongly entertained as a source of satisfaction. Tharp and Wetzel (1969) have perhaps made the most successful attempt so far to weld theory with practice in this field, and other work has been reviewed by Stumphauser (1973). The application of the principles of behaviour modification within the offender's natural environment to delinquency is still at an early stage and techniques are in need of considerable refinement, but it would undoubtedly be beneficial if an interest in this approach were to be taken by social workers and probation officers.

Lastly, the individual could be taught responses which would compete directly with the anti-social ones in his behavioural repertoire. There is a certain amount of informal evidence to suggest that some delinquent behaviour may arise either directly or indirectly from the lack of informed guidance that some individuals need in order to deal with everyday problems such as looking for a job, interacting with officials (especially the police), drawing unemployment benefit, obtaining hire purchase, or arranging for a driving test and insurance. Practical help in such matters (sometimes dignified by the term 'reality therapy') might bring about permanent changes in the individual's response to particular situations, and could constitute an important part of a broader intervention programme along environmental/learning theory lines (see, for example, Hunt & Azrin, 1973). Recent research (Dunlop, 1975; Millham et al., 1975) suggests moreover that delinquents might understand, value and co-operate in this approach.

Although these techniques (particularly the first two) involve less unselective interference in people's lives than custodial measures, they may well be seen by many as an unacceptable invasion of personal liberty because of the intensity and length of supervision they require to be exercised over the delinquent individual's life in his own environment. This is particularly the case where the assistance of modern technology is invoked for surveillance and intervention purposes (Schwitzgebel, 1971). Objections such as these require more extended discussion than can be given here since the views of both supporters and opponents of these intervention techniques illustrate the fundamental ethical problem of trying to reconcile demands for personal autonomy with the need for social control.

In the next chapter we consider the future role of institutions in the light of the environmental/learning theory of behaviour sketched out above. But before doing this it should be emphasised that this theory is clearly capable of considerably greater refinement than has been attempted here; the concepts of situation, environment and opportunity, for example, are in need of closer analysis. Moreover, the theory has applications beyond the purpose for which it has been used in this report—offering an explanation for the failure of institutional intervention—and the Home Office Research Unit has examined the extent to which environmental opportunity plays a part in particular crimes. Studies have been conducted on the effectiveness of steering-column locks, and on the extent to which supervision of passengers by crews relates to the location of damage on buses. It is hoped that further development of the theory will be possible as a result of these and other empirical studies.

CHAPTER 7

Postscript—The Future Role of Institutions

Their role in dealing with delinquents

Despite the strength of the arguments which question its effectiveness in reducing delinquent behaviour it is likely that institutional intervention will continue to be used with this purpose in mind. Because this is so, it may be useful to examine those elements in residential programmes which, if properly emphasised, might fit in with the environmental/learning approach to the reduction of delinquency outlined in the previous chapter. Mention has already been made of the need to keep absconding to a minimum and to encourage responsible behaviour in the school. In addition, the stress laid by many programmes on the acquisition of vocational and educational skills should help to ensure that on return to the outside world boys would be better equipped to take advantage of work and educational opportunities. In terms of the theory, boys would be provided with new, pro-social, responses which might be more reinforcing than the original delinquent ones. Moreover, if a boy were given the means to develop a routine of regular school or work, this would also reduce his opportunities for delinquent behaviour.

Though there is some evidence that approved schools which emphasised the acquisition of work skills had a slightly higher success rate than others—particularly when this was geared to job opportunities on release (Dunlop, 1975)—the efficiency with which these skills are taught varies greatly within the community homes system. Where they are still taught—and many schools are closing their trade departments, partly as a consequence of the raising of the school-leaving age—they may be inadequate for, or irrelevant to, subsequent employment opportunities. They are, for example, insufficiently keyed to proper apprenticeship schemes, and sometimes work is organised more to suit the somewhat limited requirements of school maintenance than to provide the more comprehensive training offered by a properly designed and developing course of instruction. Moreover, the teaching and work situations are often rather different from those to be faced by a boy on his return home; both trade departments and schoolroom, for example, can easily secure attendance—powers which do not exist in the post-institutional environment.

There are other ways too in which the approved school (or community home) is unlike ordinary schools; it admits boys within narrow age limits and possessing similar (low) educational achievements. Although staff/boy ratios are often higher than in ordinary schools, so that more attention can be paid to bringing educational attainments up to standard, the schools are too small to be able to afford those specialist staff and facilities which enable large day schools to develop educational potential further. The fact that boys come and go throughout the school year—often staying only a short while—makes it even more difficult for the schools to organise the curriculum to provide opportunities for building upon basic attainments.

We suggested in the previous chapter that although behaviours learned in the residential situation may remain more-or-less permanently in the individual's behavioural repertoire, they may not be carried over into the post-institutional environment unless it is substantially similar to the former. In the case of educational and work skills, the prerequisite of their performance may be that the individual be placed, on his release, into educational and work environments which offer him similar controls and reinforcements to those he received while in the institution. It should also be recognised that in the post-institutional environment these skills and their value as routes to reinforcement will suddenly enter into direct competition with the original reinforcers of the offender's delinquent responses. In these circumstances, if easier and proven routes to satisfaction still remain open to him, it is probably too much to expect the individual himself to seek out situations where his newly-acquired skills can be performed.

Although this objection might seem merely to emphasise the importance of planning a boy's release and aftercare, it may alternatively raise the question of whether, given the problems which have been outlined, residential programmes are the best, or only, means of providing these skills or securing their performance in the world outside the institution. Many of the necessary facilities could be provided in day schools within the boy's own community; this would by-pass most problems of carry-over and ensure that, since the skills were learned within the individual's natural setting, they would from the start be in direct competition with delinquent responses*.

Institutions also have the opportunity of putting environmental/learning theory into practice when they turn their attention to trying to modify the offender's home environment. It has been found, for instance, that a probationer's chances of re-offending very much depend on his family and, in particular, are less (a) when the father's discipline is firm; (b) the father shows affection for his son; and (c) the father is supported in his discipline by the mother (Davies & Sinclair, 1971). McMichael (1974) found that approved schoolboys at Loaningdale who had enjoyed reasonable-to-good relationships with their parents prior to committal were significantly more likely to be successful on release than those with poorer relationships. In addition, she claimed that where a reconciliation between an offender and his family occurred during the intervention process, this significantly reduced the extent of future delinquency.

Findings like these suggest that 'time out' in a residential institution could be put to better use if, during the offender's absence, efforts were made to alter

---

* We do not deny the difficulties of this approach, in terms either of ensuring that the individual takes advantages of his educational and vocational opportunities, or of providing more adequate services than exist at present. The advantages are that skills are developed in a context where their impact upon delinquency can constantly be tested and adjusted.

his home environment in ways which might not be otherwise practicable.* There is the danger that where such attempts are not made, temporary residential placement will merely become part of a recurring pattern of crisis and removal whose results will be damaging to both parents and children. At the present time, offenders are still often released from institutional programmes without any sustained effort having been made to deal with the home situation during the interval. In part this is due to a shortage of trained personnel, but a further difficulty is that even where such work is attempted on a regular and intensive basis, the influence of the medical model of intervention ensures that more attention is paid to casework with the parents than to seeking out and modifying those aspects of the family environment which elicit and maintain the delinquent responses of the child. Moreover, where it is the quality of child-parent relationships which is in question, environmental/learning theory suggests that improvements in this area cannot be made in the absence of one of the parties†, though a temporary period of separation may reduce tensions and provide the time to work out appropriate intervention strategies.

In 1970, 90% of boys leaving approved school were released to their own homes (HMSO, 1972). Though it is a widely accepted aim of institutional intervention that a child should eventually be restored to his family, it cannot be assumed that this course would inevitably secure the greatest reduction in post-institutional delinquency. When the main determinants of delinquent behaviour appear to lie in the home environment, and where it is impossible or impracticable to make changes there, it may be more realistic—either immediately, or after a trial 'time-out' period—to remove the offender to a new environment in the community. There are a number of research findings which give some support to this argument. Sinclair's (1971) probation hostel research suggested that boys who had been taken care of by more than one family were more likely to be reconvicted if sent home after release, than if sent to lodgings. Craft's (1965) study of Beech House indicated a similar (though not statistically significant) trend for boys from unsatisfactory homes to do better on release if sent to lodgings or to foster-parents, while Campbell (1965) reported that boys sent to sea from a West Country nautical school were less likely to become delinquent after release than others released to their own homes. Though it is conceivable that elements in the institutional programmes themselves may have made some contribution to these results (ie where new skills were learned, and new opportunities to exercise them provided on release) it seems more likely in the light of

---

* 'Time out' is indeed one example of the way in which a period of residential care might be used—in appropriate individual cases—to assist the sort of community-based intervention programme implicit in an environmental/learning approach to the reduction of delinquent behaviour.

† Institutional programmes often attempt to create styles of residential living assumed to be analogous to those of family life in order to compensate children for previous deprivation and to provide them with experience of satisfactory (though short-term) relationships with sympathetic adults. Improvements brought about by such periods of emotional stability are unlikely to be maintained if the child is returned to a home where parental rejection or the original sources of deprivation still exist.

earlier discussion that they occurred because the offender was transferred on release to a new environment which, perhaps, provided fewer opportunities for delinquent behaviour. McKissack (1967) has suggested that it may be just such self-imposed or unlooked-for changes in an individual's personal environment as being fostered out, marrying, or joining the armed forces, which provide a radical enough change to terminate a delinquent career. Now that further restrictions have been placed on entry to the Services there are perhaps fewer opportunities for this to occur.

Efforts at long-term pre-discharge planning on the part of institutional programmes in order to ease the offender's passage back into his own community have not always provided evidence of higher success rates than those achieved by more conventional release procedures (Hood, 1966). Once again, this is probably due to the fact that, since residential programmes concentrate on changing the offender rather than on modifying the environment to which he will return, insufficient attention is paid by pre-release programmes to the task of ensuring that the offender's post-institutional circumstances facilitate the maintenance of behaviour patterns acquired in the institution. It is possible, however, that such programmes may be more successful in maintaining any behaviour changes they are able to bring about in the residential setting if, in some way, the offender can take his institutional environment (or salient aspects of it) with him when he leaves.* Fairweather et al.'s (1969) work with mental patients, for example, suggests that some increase in the length of time during which patients stay out of hospital can be expected when it is possible to carry over into the outside community the socially supportive living situation created by the hospital and by the patients' hospital peer group, through the provision on their release of hostel accommodation and a communal work enterprise for that same peer group. His results need to be treated with some caution, however, as there appears to have been no difference in the proportions returned to hospital from the hostel and non-hostel groups. It may be the case that such ventures are only likely to be really successful so long as they provide permanent sheltered accommodation for their inmates, where a high degree of maladjusted behaviour can be tolerated, rather than the sort of temporary hostel accommodation usually provided at present.

In conclusion, it seems unlikely that institutions will make any serious impact on the reduction of juvenile delinquency while their present theoretical orientation and practice (and those of the care authority) cause them to pay insufficient attention either to factors in the offender's environment which influence delinquent behaviour, or to ways in which differences between the institutional and post-institutional setting may impede the carry-over of behaviour learned in the former. Instead a more restricted role in dealing with delinquents must be assigned to them, and this is discussed below.

---

* Institutional intervention is only justified in these circumstances if it is essential that a preliminary setting be provided in which a supporting social environment can be assembled for the clients, prior to its transplantation into the community at large.

Their other functions with respect to delinquents

When children are grossly ill-treated or neglected by their parents, they can be removed from their families and given some form of substitute care. Some of these children are also juvenile offenders, whose home circumstances were first brought to the attention of the social services when their delinquent behaviour was being investigated. Since, because of their difficult behaviour, delinquent children are often unsuitable for fostering, a residential placement is sometimes the only form of substitute care available.

Where a delinquent child is not so grossly neglected it is more difficult to justify the need for substitute care. In these circumstances the case for placing a delinquent child in residential care may rest largely on the assumption that delinquent behaviour is itself evidence of a sufficient level of parental neglect to justify the child's removal.* Quite apart from the question of whether this assumption is a tenable one, it is debatable whether in any case institutional programmes necessarily provide better care and control than the children's parents. As Millham et al. (1975)—to quote a recent study—comment, there is always the possibility, where delinquents are placed together in institutional programmes, that such a process will have the effect of mutually reinforcing delinquent tendencies and behaviour amongst the boys; and it has been argued in this report that institutions do not appear to bring about any long-term reduction in delinquency, nor do they always maintain effective supervision (see statistics on absconding in Clarke & Martin, 1971). As Wheeler et al. (1967) comment:

> '... it is not at all clear that doing something is better than doing nothing, or that doing one thing is better than doing another. This is a hard fact that simply must be faced. Indeed, we are finally beginning to understand that any intervention has the possibility of harm as well as help, and it is conceivable that the actions of even the well-meaning helpers do as much harm as good. At least in the absence of strong evidence that they are effective, there is reason to guard against intervening in the life of the child or family.'

Nevertheless, there will always be a limited need for controls to be placed on behaviour which genuinely endangers the public (or the child himself) where alternatives to custody would involve an intensity of surveillance too costly, or a risk to the public too great, to be practical. Here again, however, the absence of proven therapeutic effectiveness of current techniques of intervention makes it important that the issue should be put squarely in these terms.

In this report we have concentrated upon an examination of the effectiveness of residential intervention in reducing juvenile offenders' subsequent delinquent

---

* Under the Children and Young Persons Act 1969, a child can be made the subject of a care order (which may result in residential placement) on the grounds of his offending, provided that it can also be shown that he is in need of care and control which he is unlikely to receive if a care order is not made. Evidence of offending may also be held to go some, or even most, of the way to satisfying the 'care and control' test.

behaviour. But the sort of institutional programme which used to be provided by the approved schools (and is still provided by community homes) is also seen by the public as serving both as a punishment to the delinquent and a general deterrent to the potential wrongdoer—even though not officially designed for or recognised as fulfilling such purposes. Further discussion of these other functions is beyond the scope of this report, though it should be borne in mind that any importance they may have is in no way diminished by evidence that residential intervention programmes are of little rehabilitative value. To dismantle the apparatus of institutional intervention without adequate discussion and analysis of the role institutions of this kind may play in the process of social control, by reducing the likelihood that a non-offender will commit his first delinquent act, would be hazardous. The extent to which institutions can or do perform the functions of care, custody and deterrence satisfactorily (or indeed cost-effectively) should now be the subject of empirical investigation.

APPENDIX 1

Changes in the Research Design

The original research was rather more ambitious than the project which was finally implemented. Firstly, it had been thought advisable to incorporate a lengthy 'flushing-out' period in the design, so that the early batch of randomly-allocated boys—who would have had contact with boys admitted to the E and C Houses before the experiment began—could be discarded from the analysis of results. It was also thought that this would afford a quiescent period during which the E House could develop its methods without feeling under pressure to codify its practices prematurely. Secondly, provision was made for the administration of a battery of psychological tests to the boys, immediately before their admission to the school and shortly before release. Lastly, it had been planned to describe the two regimes in as much detail as possible. These aspects of the original design had either to be extensively modified or abandoned because of subsequent developments; some of these are described below.

Decline in admissions

The decline in admissions of 'eligible' boys to the school during the course of the controlled trial has been fully discussed elsewhere (Clarke & Cornish, 1972). The main reason for the decline was that the classifying school became increasingly reluctant to send boys to a school where, because of random allocation, they might not receive the form of treatment or training which had been considered most appropriate for them. The decline unacceptably extended the duration of the research and, in consequence, led to the premature abandonment of random allocation in October 1969. To compensate for the resulting limitation in the sample size, it was decided to include data on those boys who had been in the E and C Houses during the 'flushing-out' period, even though this might somewhat weaken the design. Since the last boys not subject to random allocation had left the two Houses as late as 1967, the exclusion of boys randomly-allocated up until then would have entailed a loss to the E and C House samples of 41, and 49 boys, respectively.*

Owing to the observance earlier in the research of the 'flushing-out' period (which had itself been longer than originally intended because of the decline in admissions) plans for detailed pre- and post-intervention testing programmes had not been implemented until the beginning of 1968. (At this time the research project received the assistance of an additional member of staff). The cutback in numbers of boys together with considerations of the cost of continuing to

---

* The decline in admissions, coupled with a relatively constant average length of stay for the boys in both houses, had the effect of maintaining numbers actually taking part in the programmes at a very satisfactory level as regards staff/boy ratios. Had numbers on roll been fewer and turnover more rapid, however, both regimes might have suffered from having no relatively stable core of experienced members to maintain and hand on the traditions of their programme.

give extensive psychological tests to the boys, led to the decision to abandon the testing programme altogether. The tests selected had been designed to provide information relating to possible attitude and personality change in the boys during their stay in the E and C Houses. In particular it was hoped that the inclusion of the Jesness Inventory and a specially-designed Osgood Semantic Differential in the battery of tests would provide some form of intermediate criteria (see Chapter 4) by which to measure programme success, and their omission from the final research design might be seen by some as a serious defect. Those working on the research, however, had become disillusioned with the concept of personality and with the notion of personality and attitude testing (see Chapter 6). At about the time when it had to be decided whether or not to continue with the testing programme, some results became available (subsequently published, cf. Mott, 1973), which cast considerable doubt on the value of the Jesness Inventory—a test which had been specially designed for use in evaluating programmes for delinquents. Quite apart from cost, it seemed highly questionable to continue with a component of the research which was unlikely to produce useful results.

The detailed studies of regime variables were also curtailed—in particular, the use of critical incident techniques (Flanagan, 1954) to investigate which aspects of boys' behaviour seemed most important to staff in the E and C Houses, the development of methods for looking at staff/boy verbal interaction during house meetings, and the implementation of sociometric investigations. It was difficult to justify continuing with this detailed work when the project as a whole had been severely cut.* Moreover, evidence was gradually accumulating from other research about the ineffectiveness of residential intervention, and there seemed little point in describing very carefully two regimes which were likely to prove similarly ineffective. Even if differences in effectiveness were found it became increasingly obvious that detailed description of the regimes would do no more than multiply the possible explanations for the source of these differences, rather than enable a decision between competing alternatives to be made.†

Other threats to the continuation of the research

The decline in admissions and the consequent overcrowding of the Third House (see Chapter 4) caused many difficulties for the school's senior staff. On the one hand the research workers pressed them to ask the classifying school to allocate more 'eligible' boys to the school while the classifying school, in its turn,

---

* Since few research techniques relating to the descriptions of process were available at the time the research began, the curtailment of this aspect of the project was from this point of view regrettable. A very recent publication (Tizard, Sinclair & Clarke, 1975) does, however, collect together a considerable amount of current research concerned with the systematic description of regimes in institutions for children.

† 'Contrary to what had been hoped for initially, the main effect of the study of process was simply to make clearer the very many ways in which the houses differed in addition to preferred treatment technique, and therefore to proliferate possible alternative explanations for any differences in results.' (Clarke & Cornish, 1972, p. 15).

wished the school to take all boys allocated there, whether acceptable to the E House or not. Added to this, the senior staff were faced with timetabling difficulties and other administrative inconveniences created by the E House's requirement for two house meetings and one staff meeting per day, and by worries—not in the event borne out by answers to a staff questionnaire administrated in 1968—that the presence of the therapeutic community might be causing considerable strain and hostility among staff. Mention has already been made of the invidious position in which senior staff were placed by criticisms of the physical condition of the E House.* These difficulties frequently gave rise to uncertainty about the future of the house which was as much a source of anxiety to the research workers as to its staff.

There were other threats to the morale of the research workers at Kingswood: (1) the measures taken to ensure the continuation of the experiment often had to be at the expense of the original design; (2) it became clearer day-by-day that the results would be difficult to interpret; and (3) even if interpretable, the findings would only add to those already becoming available about the ineffectiveness of residential programmes. Such problems which augment each other and progressively call into question the usefulness of the research are, of course, the more serious the longer a project continues. Yet rarely does their discussion in research reports reflect the degree to which they absorb and sap the vitality of the research effort. What is more, how many research projects have never reached the report stage because of these kinds of problems?

---

* Senior staff had responsibility both for trying to maintain the E House in existence, and for the welfare of the rest of the school. Conflicts and misunderstanding arose, (a) when they felt that the E House was departing from its original programme, and (b) where they felt the research was disrupting the school as a whole. One such anxiety on the part of senior staff was that the system of random allocation, which had usurped the powers of the headmaster to allocate boys to the house he considered most suitable to their needs, would interfere with prospects for the boys' successful rehabilitation. This fear proved to be unfounded; when the reconviction rates of two groups of boys—(a) those who went into the house which the headmaster would have selected (N=48), and, (b) those who did not (N=50)—were compared, no differences were found.

APPENDIX 2

Differences Between E and C Houses

Staffing

For the purpose of the controlled trial it was clearly necessary that the staff running the two regimes should be comparable. At the beginning of the experiment, the E House had five members of staff—three full-time house staff known as 'community workers' (one of whom had duties in the school as well), a teacher on extraneous duties, and a temporary non-resident housemother. In addition, during the first half of the research, the E House benefitted from the advice and assistance of the school's clinical psychologist who had set up the therapeutic community. The C House had a housemaster, a resident housemother (his wife) and three extraneous duties staff. While these staffing ratios were numerically equivalent and gave similar coverage for 'official' supervisory duties, the use of community workers in the E house gave the latter a greater administrative capability for dealing with matters concerning the boys' welfare, both in the house itself, and in connection with their homes and after-care. In the C house most of such work was carried out by the housemaster alone, in accordance with traditional approved school practice.

The differences in staffing and staff duties reflected the houses' respective emphases on different aspects of the intervention process and on the initial needs associated with the development of a new type of regime; as the research proceeded, however, these differences became attenuated with the departure of the clinical psychologist, and the addition of an extra housemaster to the C House's complement.

The exigencies of staff turnover meant that from time to time one or other of the houses was short-staffed. During the period in which random allocation operated however, there were no significant differences between the houses in staff turnover; in the E House the average length of stay was 18·6 months (s.d.=13·3) while in the C House it was 20·1 months (s.d.=15·2).

The different staffing policies of the two houses were reflected in differences in qualifications, experience and age. During the earlier part of the controlled trial, three members of the E House staff had child-care or social work qualifications while the C House contained none. By 1968, the E House still had the only two house staff with residential child care qualifications, together with one further member of staff, whose experience of social work was in the probation service. When further education (including teacher-training) was considered the C House made a slightly better showing. In terms of experience in residential work, however, the two houses were similar.

The mean age of members of staff in the E House tended to be lower than that of the C House; in 1968 it was 39 years for the E House and 49 years for the C House. Though these differences were not significant they were in the expected direction, given that the E House was running a new form of approved school regime.

It was important for the research that from the outset staff in E and C Houses should be in sympathy with the aims of their house; as far as the C House was concerned there were few problems since the house team had been together and engaged in running this traditional regime for the previous ten years. Owing to staff vacancies in the E House, its programme was able to start out with a new house team whose staff were chosen for their interest in the venture. A policy of appointing only those in sympathy with the respective aims of the two houses was largely maintained during the course of the research.

General attitudes to intervention

When, in 1968, the time came to examine the two regimes more closely, questionnaires were constructed to examine staff ideologies and attitudes. The first (34-item) questionnaire was based, with suitable modifications, on the 'Custodial Mental Illness Ideology Scale' (See Gilbert and Levinson, 1957; revised by Street et al., 1966). This was intended to measure the extent to which the staff could be characterised as holding 'training' as opposed to 'treatment' attitudes towards their charges.

Comparison of scores obtained from members of E House ($N=8$) and C House ($N=10$) teams over a two-year period showed that E House staff were significantly more 'treatment' orientated than C House staff (Man-Whitney 'U' Test: $p < \cdot 01$).*

Further analysis, using scores obtained by Third House staff ($N=13$) and senior staff ($N=6$) showed that the C House's 'training' ideology was shared by the rest of the school. A Ryan's Mann-Whitney Multiple Comparison showed the E House to be significantly different from both C House and the Third House, while the C House scores were similar to those of the latter. Moreover, the mean scores for the senior management staff were found to be similar to those of C House and the Third House. Differences between senior staff and E House scores almost reached statistical significance at the $\cdot 05$ level, but small numbers in the former sample may have precluded satisfactory statistical comparison.

A second questionnaire, based on the Staff Questionnaire produced by Street et al. (1966), was used in a more detailed examination of staff attitudes to various aspects of approved school work. The first question asked staff to choose, from a set of six statements about approved school aims, those two which they thought best represented (a) the actual aims of their house, and (b) the aims which they themselves wished to see implemented. The six statements were grouped (though randomly-presented) into three pairs, descriptive of three types of orientation—

---

* E and C House scores on two sub-scales of the questionnaire—'Discipline' and 'Understanding'—were also found to be significantly different. These results, while in line with avowed E House policies on these matters, are not emphasised since the sub-scales were made up of very few items (cf. Street et al., 1966).

'custodial', 'training', and 'treatment'. Analysis of the answers showed that E House staff were unanimous in choosing the 'treatment' pair for both actual and desired aims—an indication of a high degree of staff cohesiveness. There was, however, little agreement among staff in the C House in their choices with respect to desired and actual aims. The E House staff also believed—significantly more often than those in the C House—that the aims they had selected as being desirable were, in fact, being implemented by the house (Fisher's Exact Test: $p < \cdot 01$). This further indicated their consciousness of working as a team with a shared identity.

The comparative lack of agreement amongst staff in the C House concerning actual or desired aims may reflect both the fact that the C House staff group worked less as a team sharing common objectives after the departure of the original housemaster, and that traditional approved school methods of intervention were themselves undergoing some questioning by this time. The findings probably do not indicate any serious dissatisfaction amongst C House staff; questioned later whether they would like to work in another house, only two of the ten members of staff indicated that they would. None of the E House staff wanted to do so.

Staff attitudes on particular policy issues

The four principles of democratization, permissiveness, communalism, and reality confrontation could be expected to guide E House staff policy concerning such issues as, for example, allocating pocket money, awarding weekend leave, and dealing with absconding and other problems of communal living.

On the other hand, C House policy was broadly determined by the 'Rewards and Privileges Scheme' drawn up for the school in 1964 by the headmaster. In this scheme pocket money, weekend ('privilege') leave and certain other minor privileges, were tied to boys' progress through three grades. Following discussion at house level, grade meetings attended by staff and boys were held by the headmaster at monthly intervals, boys' conduct being reviewed to determine whether promotion or demotion was necessary. The scheme (which for the most part was rejected by the E House staff as a basis for their programme) also laid down punishments such as fines, extra duties, or loss of privileges for failure to carry out domestic duties satisfactorily, for damaging property, and for breaking rules such as those governing smoking and unauthorised absence from the school. These sanctions were again outlined in a later document directed to the C House in 1968 when the original housemaster left.

Items included in the second staff questionnaire were designed to reveal differences in attitudes towards:

    (a) the degree of control needed in dealing with the boys;
    (b) the extent to which peer-group influences should be utilized;
    (c) the degree of closeness to be developed in staff/boy relations;
    (d) the awarding of pocket money;

(e) the role of housemothers in approved schools;
(f) home leave;
(g) the organisation of leisure activities;
(h) absconding and corporal punishment.

The respondent was again asked to select, from a number of alternative statements chosen to reflect 'custodial', 'training' or 'treatment' orientations, the one which most closely approached his own views about the topic under consideration.

Staff from the two houses (for C House, N=10, for E, N=8) differed little in their responses to individual items of policy; out of eleven questions the two groups differed significantly only with regard to one—their opinions about the degree of control it was necessary to exercise over their charges. Here the C House unaminously favoured a 'training' viewpoint (Fisher's Exact Test: $p = < \cdot 02$).

Since, however, the answers to the eleven questions revealed a consistent trend on the part of the E House staff to favour answers in the 'treatment' direction, a 'policy-orientation scale' was constructed using the questions, together with a question on treatment aims. The E House staff were found to obtain scores which were significantly more 'treatment' orientated than those of the C House (Mann–Whitney 'U' Test: $p = < \cdot 02$).

A further question invited respondents to rate whether they thought 'too little', 'about right' or 'too much' attention was paid by the school as a whole to certain aspects of approved school programmes. These included 'training' items on work habits, trade skills, educational abilities, manners, obedience and personal hygiene, together with 'treatment' items on learning to understand the behaviour and points of view of others, learning to cope with anti-authority feelings, developing individual talents, and learning how to mix with ordinary young people outside the school. Answers to individual items revealed little difference between the houses*, but scores on a 'too-much-training' scale assembled from individual items showed that the E House staff considered that too much emphasis was placed on 'training' in the school as a whole (Mann–Whitney 'U' Test: $p = < \cdot 05$).

As a further method of checking on staff attitudes, respondents were presented with a list of 16 types of boys' behaviour commonly causing difficulties in house situations, and asked to choose and arrange five of these in order of seriousness. There were some similarities in the results, bullying, anxiety and tenseness, damage and dishonesty appearing to be common features of both regimes. C House staff, however, seemed to find anti-authority attitudes their main problem, while for the E House, attention was focussed on solitariness and withdrawal

---

* Significantly more E House staff, however, felt that too little emphasis was placed on helping boys to understand other boys' behaviour and points of view—an important element of reality confrontation (Fisher's Exact Test: $p = < \cdot 02$).

from the life of the house. Disobedience and aggression to staff were never seen as problems by E House staff, rudeness and swearing, rarely so.

In summary, answers to the second staff questionnaire indicate that, just as staff in the E House were more 'treatment' orientated in their general ideology, so they were significantly more 'treatment' orientated in their attitude to particular policy issues.

Staff practice
Descriptions of intervention programmes and staff attitudes are no substitute for evidence that what is described is being put into practice. In the absence of supporting information, there is no guarantee that data on staff attitudes have not been contaminated by the respondent's knowledge of what he thinks the questioner would like to hear, or of what attitudes are currently fashionable in the residential child care field.

(a) Degree of house autonomy and staff rules:
Arguments were sometimes voiced by staff that since the E House was operating within a school whose senior staff held more conventional views about approved school work* it might not have been able to exercise sufficient autonomy in policy matters (see Chapter 4). The E House was bound to some extent by the Rewards and Privileges Scheme, particularly in circumstances where it was felt either that the issue was a school rather than a house affair or that, in the interests of the school, boys in the E House should be treated on the same footing as the rest. For instance, the E House were prevented by the Approved School Rules from exercising control over the date of a boy's discharge from the House. This was the responsibility of the school's managers, guided by reports from the senior and house staff. Other factors too, such as the availability of a suitable job, and the practice of releasing boys to coincide with holiday periods, may have served to depress variability between the houses in this respect, the average length of stay for E House boys being, throughout the experiment, 13·4 months (s.d.=5·7), and for the C House, 13·6 months (s.d.=6·0).

By and large, however, the E House was still given considerable latitude to develop its own policies. In an attempt to implement the principles of democratization and communalism the house sought to blur the distinctions in status and function amongst the staff team, much as the Henderson Hospital had tried to flatten the administrative hierarchy in their unit. Efforts in this direction varied at different points in the experiment. Of the original founder the headmaster of the day commented in a report to the Managers that: 'There is no doubt in my mind that

---

* Responses from the second staff questionnaire showed senior staff to be significantly less 'treatment' orientated than E House staff. No significant differences were found between the scores of senior staff and C House staff, and this bears out the earlier findings which showed similar mean scores for C House, Third House, and senior staff on the first questionnaire.

he is very much the leader and driving force in the community and that boys and staff recognise this'. A system of 'multiple leadership' was proposed at this time to avoid any one member of staff becoming the focus of boys' attention and was more fully put into practice later. In the C House, staff roles were more clearly differentiated, the housemaster having sole responsibility both for the administrative work of the house and, though he acted after consultation with his extraneous duties staff, for house policy.

(b) House meetings and leave passes:
As previously discussed, the E House developed their twice daily house meetings as a means for sharing responsibility, involving the boys in treatment, and improving communications. The C House also held daily meetings, but the form these took was very different; while participants in the E House meetings sat in a circle, boys and staff mingling freely and raising issues without distinction of status, in the C House boys were arranged in rows of chairs facing staff and took little part in the proceedings (this arrangement was relaxed in the latter period of the controlled trial). These meetings were directed, and largely monopolised, by staff. Content was usually limited to the giving of information, to criticisms of poor behaviour, and to urging the boys to maintain house standards.

During 1968 both houses used small group meetings held by a member of staff to determine the giving of 'privilege' leave passes. Procedures were similar; boys would report on the behaviour of candidates for leave passes (usually on the basis of their performance at domestic duties) and observations and recommendations would be entered on the leave pass. The pass would then go either before the main house meeting (in the E House) or to the house staff (in the C House) for further comment. The forms would then be sent to the headmaster, who had the ultimate responsibility for granting or withholding leave.

Despite these formal similarities, striking differences between the houses were revealed when the leave pass forms were analysed in more detail. In line with their policy of involving boys in decision-making it was found that in the E House no less than 122 out of 141 passes granted within a six-month period contained comments written by the boys themselves: none were written by staff, the other 19 passes containing no comments. Of written comments from leave pass groups in the C House, however, 105 out of 136 were written by staff (20 out of the remaining 31 had no comments).

Although the headmaster had final control of leave pass allocations, he did not, on the whole, interfere with the E House policy in this matter, except to ensure that the amounts of leave given to the two Houses were substantially the same. The amount of senior staff intervention can be gauged from their entries on the leave passes themselves; although they commented about boys' behaviour and other matters on passes from both houses, those from the E House received significantly fewer comments than those of the C House (Chi-square $=8.8$; d.f.1, $p<.005$).

(c) Management of boys:

In the E House, a policy of discussion rather than coercion was used in matters such as getting up in the mornings and the allocation of domestic duties. This policy, although sometimes criticised by senior staff because of its effects on routine house management, continued throughout the controlled trial on the grounds that the permissiveness afforded to the boys was diagnostically and therapeutically valuable.

Similarly, again in line with the principle of communalism, boys were allowed to address members of staff by their first names, or nicknames, and were able to decide for themselves with whom they shared bedrooms and tables at mealtimes. In contrast, C House arrangements were more formal; staff were addressed as 'Mr' and mealtime and bedroom places could only be changed by special request to the housemaster.

In the C House, pocket money was related to a boy's conduct grade, while the E House adopted a flat-rate pocket money system with two levels, depending on how long a boy had been in the house. Thus although expenditure on pocket money was the same for both houses, the E House omitted any element of individual incentive.

(d) Caning:

Since it was part of E House policy to allow some degree of overtly deviant behaviour in the belief that 'acting out' would be therapeutically beneficial, it could be expected that they would regard absconding in a rather less serious light than more traditional regimes. In fact, as we have seen, staff attitudes to absconding showed no significant differences. The E House were, however, anxious that punishment for absconding should be avoided as far as possible. In accordance with the Approved School Rules only the headmaster or—in his absence—a member of the senior staff acting as headmaster could administer the cane and they made little use of it during the course of the controlled trial. In E and C Houses a total of only 24 boys were caned—8 in the E House and 16 in the C House, an indication that E House internal policy towards the punishment of absconding was taken into consideration by senior staff. Caning as a punishment for other infractions was used for C House boys (25 instances) more than for E House boys (16 instances); these figures, however, conceal larger variations between houses in the use of corporal punishment at different periods of the research. During 1967 and 1968, for example, only one boy was caned in the E House, as against 17 boys in the C House.

(e) Contact with home:

An important element in the E House programme was its emphasis on maintaining and strengthening boys' contacts with their homes and after-care officers, whilst they were still at the school. Both E and C Houses used the services of probation officers and child care officers, the E House favouring the former, and

C House, the latter (Chi-square=14·0; d.f.1, p<·001)*. It was not possible to control this source of variation between the two houses, but in the light of current evidence about the infrequency of after-care visits (McMichael, 1974), and in view of the fact that there was no difference in reconviction rates between the two groups of boys supervised by the different kind of after-care officer, perhaps not too much significance should be accorded to it.

Home leave was governed largely by Home Office rules and for this reason, although official policy changed by degrees during the research in the direction of granting more leave, there were no significant differences between the mean numbers of *days* leave given to boys in each house (E House mean=57·7 days, s.d. 39·5; C House mean=50·0, s.d. 30·4). It was, however, notable that E House boys managed to get rather more than a week's extra leave, and that the amount of leave given to individual boys showed rather more variability. Very similar results emerged when the mean number of separate leave *periods* given were analysed. Since the E House considered home leave as an essential part of the programme, to be given as and when required, and for different periods of time, this variability may reflect the extent to which the E House were able to adapt leave regulations to their own requirements.

In order to look at various aspects of house policy and boys' behaviour, E and C Houses were asked to complete a daily log over a seven-month period during 1968–9. Although it was recognised that any differences found between the houses might merely reflect differences in willingness or conscientiousness to record information, it was felt that a reliance on data which were relatively objective and easy to collect would, together with regular supervisory checks on the records by one of the research workers, reduce such sources of error.

One of the entries related to the frequency of staff journeys outside the house in order to work with the home. During the period under consideration no significant differences in the frequency of such visits were found between the two houses. When visits made to each of the houses by outsiders were considered, however, a different picture emerged, E House receiving significantly more visitors per month than the C House even when adjustment had been made for the slightly higher numbers in the E House (Mann–Whitney 'U' Test: p<·02). As it was felt that some of these visits might be due to the novelty of the experimental programme, a further analysis of the data was made to distinguish (a) visits made to see the house and (b) visits made to see individual children by families, friends or after-care officers. When the former group was omitted it was still found that the E House received twice as many visitors as the C House (Mann–Whitney 'U' Test: p<·02), indicating that the former seemed to be maintaining greater contact with the home.†

---

* It was the school's policy to use child care officers in preference to probation officers in view of the way national policy was moving.
† It was also found that significantly more visitors came to the E House to see the experimental programme in operation than came to the C House. Since this might have produced Hawthorne effects steps were taken to correct this state of affairs (Clarke & Cornish, 1972).

Boys behaviour in the houses

Since staff attitudes and many aspects of policy were clearly different in the two houses, it was expected that differences would be found in boys' behaviour. Several methods were used to gather data relevant to this—further entries in the daily log, records of damage to the houses and to clothing, and absconding data.

(a) Damage and theft:

Staff were asked to make an entry in the daily log each time damage to house furniture or fittings was noticed. As a result it was found that during the period under consideration a total of 128 incidents were reported by E House staff, as against 70 by the C House. This difference was not significant when adjustment was made for differences between the mean numbers of boys in the two houses during this period (E House 20 boys, C House 16).

A measure of damage which was not so likely to be affected by differences in reporting practices between the houses was provided by records of window breakages, which had been kept by the school's maintenance department for a considerable number of years. Records for the four complete years (1960–63) before the establishment of the new regime in the E House showed the rate of breakages there (number broken=215) to be nearly twice that of the C House (number broken=121). During the first four completed years after (1965–8) the E House rate of breakages (403) had become nearly four times as great as that of the C House (125), whose rate remained steady throughout the two periods (Chi-square=14·75; d.f.1, $p < \cdot 001$). Because of the nature of the comparison, the findings could not be explained in terms of E House's greater exposure to damage in the later period, since no relevant alterations had been made to the house which might have increased its vulnerability in that respect. The most likely explanation of the findings would seem to be that the E House encouraged 'acting-out' behaviour which led to an increase in the numbers of windows broken.

Since the encouragement of 'acting-out' might be expected to increase the amount of horseplay and fighting in the E House, records kept by the school's sewing room (over a ten-month period in 1968–9) of damage to boys' clothing were examined. The two Houses were not found to differ significantly in this respect. Analysis of the number of thefts recorded as being committed in each house over a six month period similarly failed to reveal any differences between the two houses.

(b) Offences committed during the boys' stay at Kingswood:

83 boys from the total sample (N=280) committed offences for which they were found guilty by a court during their stay at Kingswood. Practically all these offences were committed in the outside community, while absconding or on leave. There were no differences between E and C Houses in the numbers committing

offences (21 and 19, respectively) but boys from the Third House committed significantly more (43) than the other two (Chi-square=8·4; d.f.1, p< ·005).

On a more general point, it should be noted that from the total sample it was found that those who offended while at Kingswood were more likely to be reconvicted afterwards (Chi-square=4·24; d.f.1, p< ·05). This association did not hold for the individual houses. Although information about offences committed while at school may well be a useful measure of 'acting-out' and be of some small predictive value with regard to future delinquent behaviour, it is not so 'pure' a measure as absconding, since information about the former is both less complete and, perhaps, more influenced by administrative factors such as the decision whether or not to prosecute.

(c) Absconding:

It has been argued (Sinclair and Clarke, 1973) that absconding can be regarded as a measure of 'acting-out' within an institution. The difference in the numbers of boys absconding from the two houses was not significant (E House, 58 absconders; C House, 54), but there were more *incidents* of absconding from the therapeutic community—222 as compared with 170 in the C House. These differences were largely accounted for, however, by the very few boys who absconded seven or more times. There were six such boys in the C House who committed a total of 56 abscondings, whereas the E House had nine, responsible between them for 95 abscondings. This would seem to be evidence, consistent with stated treatment philosophy, of a greater tolerance of absconding by the E House*.

Further detailed analysis of absconding patterns revealed a number of other small differences between the houses. These will not be described in detail since it is difficult to disentangle the possible explanations for them. For instance, throughout the research there appeared to be a comparatively steady rate of absconding from the therapeutic community, whereas the C House had quite long periods free from absconding punctuated by absconding peaks and even by what, at first, appeared to be 'epidemics' of absconding.† This, together with evidence that abscondings from the therapeutic community were more often lone, day-time, and short-lived affairs, suggested that the E House boys were less affected by opportunity factors than those in the C House, and that they regarded absconding as an approved method of dealing with boredom, frustration, and anxiety. This, nevertheless was somewhat belied by sharper absconding peaks for the E House at particular times of the year, (January, August and September),

---

* 20 boys absconded seven or more times from the Third House, committing between them 227 abscondings. Although the percentage of boys absconding from the Third House was the same as from the other two, the greater number of incidents (372) for which they were collectively responsible is another indication of the difficulties faced by the Third House.

† Several distinct 'epidemics' of absconding were identified in the C House by means of a Markov process analysis. Closer examination of these revealed, however, that they were largely accounted for by small groups of boys absconding repeatedly, rather than by large numbers of boys absconding once or twice.

and on certain days of the week (Mondays and Tuesdays). Again, it could not be decided on the basis of the available data how far these peaks were accounted for by more boys failing to return from leave (especially as to some extent it may also have been consequent upon the slightly more liberal and individualized policy of granting leave in the E House).

(c) Enuresis:

Since it has often been claimed that living in a therapeutic community imposes quite severe strain on boys, an attempt was made to find out whether differences in enuretic behaviour (often considered a symptom of anxiety and tension) existed between the two houses. Differences were found to exist, but seemed to point to a greater incidence of enuresis in the C House (163 incidents were recorded in the C House over a six-month period as against 71 incidents in the E House, when the latter's figures were adjusted for its larger numbers on roll). When the information was examined in more detail, however, it was found that 74% (121) of the episodes in the C House were attributable to two boys, both enuretics of long standing. There were, in fact, equal numbers of boys (7) in both Houses who were recorded as being enuretic at some time.

(d) Friendship patterns:

As part of a questionnaire*, constructed in 1969 to assess boys' attitudes to the house programmes in which they were participating, members of E and C Houses were asked to state which three boys in the school they liked best; it was hoped in this way to obtain data by which the patterns of interaction amongst members of the two houses might be compared. Analysis of the findings indicated the E and C Houses contained the same numbers of unchosen individuals, and of mutual pairs. Inspection of the sociograms revealed no readily interpretable differences in patterns of friendships or communication, such as might have been expected from the E House's emphasis on communalism. Other traditional indices used in sociometry such as those defining the overchosen or underchosen, group cohesion or integration showed no differences between houses. A small difference was found between the relative numbers of boys chosen from outside their own house by E and C House boys, the latter choosing more boys from other houses, but this did not reach significance†.

---

* Both the questionnaire and the sociometry were necessary simplifications of earlier and more comprehensive proposals.

† Grygier (1975) proposes a measure of 'treatment potential' based on the correlation between a boy's behaviour as seen by the staff and his popularity among his peers. The higher this correlation, it is claimed, the greater the treatment potential of the regime. In a separate exercise, boys were asked to rate how much they liked each boy in the house and members of house staff were asked to rate each boy's response to training. (This was defined as being the general response of the boy to the regime afforded by the House). Ratings were made on 5-point scales, and the correlation between the mean rating for each boy on the two dimensions was 0·41 for the E House and 0·47 for the C House, indicating little difference between the houses in 'treatment potential'.

Boys' attitudes to the regimes

A 58-item questionnaire was administered to E and C House boys in order to examine whether their perceptions about the school and their respective houses differed. Questions covered the following topics, some of which had also been included in the second staff questionnaire:

(1) boys' assessments of the school's aims;
(2) their satisfaction with the school and their own house;
(3) their opinions about the relative emphasis placed by the school on various aspects of its programme: leisure, educational and vocational training, development of social skills, development of insight, etc.;
(4) their agreement or disagreement with a list of descriptive propositions about life in the house, attitudes of staff, friendliness and cohesiveness of the peer-group, and the way the house was run;
(5) what topics the respondent talked to staff about;
(6) the influence of various groups, boys and staff, in making rules for the house;
(7) the best way of behaving when in the house;
(8) how staff in the house usually acted;
(9) the degree of freedom given to boys in their house;
(10) personal prognosis of future delinquency.

Although the questions were chosen to illustrate the influence of 'treatment' and 'training' standpoints in the respective houses, results indicated that boys seemed to hold broadly similar views on all these topics, regardless of the house in which they found themselves. Responses by E and C House boys differed significantly on only three items; asked to describe life in their house, more C House boys thought that their house had too many rules and regulations (Chi-square=$5\cdot57$; d.f.1, $p<\cdot025$); fewer of the C House boys talked to staff about 'daily work like house-cleaning and domestic duties' (Chi-square=$3\cdot96$; d.f.1, p. $<\cdot05$); and more E House boys felt that they had a lot of influence in making rules for their house (Chi-square=$6\cdot54$, d.f.1, $p<\cdot025$). More C than E House boys thought that the headmaster and deputies had a lot of influence in making house rules, but this result just failed to reach significance.

Bearing in mind the large number of comparisons made, these results must be treated with some caution, though they do suggest that the E House policy of permissiveness and shared responsibility was given some recognition by its boys. Perhaps the most striking finding is that the perceptions of the boys in the two houses should be so similar, but it cannot be determined whether this was because life under the two regimes did not differ greatly for the boys (or was very similar in those aspects they considered important—and this may tie in with the discussion in Chapter 4), or whether it was due to inadequate formulation of questions.

APPENDIX 3

Staffs' Own Evaluation of their Effectiveness

Where practitioners are unwilling to come to terms with the implications of negative research findings this cannot simply be put down to disagreements with research workers over issues such as the selection of appropriate success criteria or the extent to which intervention programmes have been adequately implemented (see Chapter 4). Practitioners characteristically believe that they are doing their job with some measure of success, and it may be that research workers' lack of attention to the evidence upon which this conviction is based has exacerbated misunderstandings between the two groups.

Staff, as we have seen, are often critical of the criteria used by research workers to measure effectiveness; this criticism arises not only from the belief that the wrong things are being measured (a point of view which, we have argued, pays little attention to the practical purposes of institutional intervention) but from a more general objection that results which show programmes to be ineffective tend also to imply that nothing is being done during the boys' stay in the institution. Staff would have many grounds for rejecting such an implication. Firstly, they actually have some success with certain problems—those, for example, in the areas of health and education. When boys put on weight, improve their reading attainments, or can be taken off tranquillising drugs, the satisfaction of achieving such tangible successes may well give staff the impression that the residential programme itself is successful, even though few such problems have a direct bearing on delinquent behaviour or demand institutional treatment in their own right.

Secondly, the schools have recently been encouraged to think of their job as primarily one of making and working through relationships, and satisfaction with this case-work approach is reinforced by the fact that staff do make mutually rewarding relationships with some boys.* Indeed, it would be surprising if the majority of children when removed from their home environment, and deprived of dependent relationships with parents, adults and other friends, did not try to re-create such relationships with available adults.

Thirdly, many children arrive at residential institutions a considerable time after they have been removed from their homes. Often they are admitted to the approved school in a disturbed state, and their behaviour in such circumstances may be attributed to deep-seated and long-standing maladjustment, rather than being seen as a normal reaction to the prolonged period of uncertainty about their future. The gradual process of settling into the new environment may be

---

* Where intervention programmes are explicitly based on these conceptions, as was the case with the E House, such relationships will be seen to have a special significance; this may account in part for the fact that E House staff, in answer to a question requesting them to assess the likely prognosis for their boys, were significantly more optimistic than staff in the C House (Mann-Whitney 'U' Test: $p < \cdot 01$).

misinterpreted by staff as evidence of therapeutic effectiveness, when in fact it represents something of a return to pre-committal levels of adjustment.

Much of what passes for 'treatment' in institutions can also more properly be regarded as being concerned with reducing the ill-effects of residential living itself. For example, while there is little evidence about the long-term effectiveness of organising programmes according to offender/programme typologies, there is some reason to believe that this eases problems of control within the institution itself (Warren, 1971). Again, the speed at which institutional adjustment is achieved and the ease by which it is maintained (boys often claim, and are seen to be, happy in their schools—Dunlop, 1975; Millham et al., 1975), can be improved by techniques of group work which are characteristically described as 'treatment' rather than inmate management; in such cases it is easy for success in the management task to be confused with progress in 'treatment'.

A further source of the conviction that a residential programme is successful comes from a belief in the efficacy of change. When innovations in an institution are made, for whatever reason, they may come to be regarded as guarantors of increased therapeutic effectiveness. But changes are often more concerned with administrative convenience than with programme improvement and even where the latter is the aim, staff may over-emphasise the real importance of the innovations made, or the changes may be semantic rather than actual. Furthermore, the difficulty of institutional change (Mathieson, 1967) may lead staff to expect correspondingly substantial improvements in effectiveness.

Residential staff, too (like all of us), have well-developed techniques for rationalising failure which also encourage resistance to negative research findings (cf. Kassebaum et al., 1971, pp. 313–317). Thus, boys who do not do well at school are described as 'very maladjusted' or 'not placed correctly' and the blame for their failure is shifted to the courts, the assessment centres, the family, or the boy himself. Absconders, the most visible failures of the system, are very often labelled in this way, even though research—far from confirming the existence of absconders as a sub-group distinguished by particular personality attributes—tends to emphasise the role played by the school environment in eliciting absconding (Clarke & Martin, 1971). Moreover, the schools often describe themselves as having increasingly become society's last resort for a hard core of delinquents created by the tariff system of sentencing*, and there is some basis for this view. This century has seen the progressive administrative differentiation of delinquents into groups requiring more or less intervention, according to their histories and family backgrounds. Yet the conclusion to be drawn is perhaps not that schools are being robbed of those whose behaviour they can improve but that, once deprived of those who can as successfully be dealt with by less drastic curtailments of personal liberty, the schools are unable to deal effectively with the remainder.

---

* This belief often co-exists with its opposite—that there is not much difference between the inmates of approved schools, children's homes or schools for the maladjusted.

REFERENCES

Adams, S	1961	'Interaction between individual interview therapy and treatment amenability in older Youth Authority wards.' In, *Inquiries concerning Kinds of Treatments for Kinds of Delinquents.* Monograph No. 2, Board of Corrections, California.
Bailey, W C	1966	'Correctional outcome: an evaluation of 100 reports.' *Journal of Criminal Law, Criminology, and Police Science,* **57,** 153–160.
Bandura, A	1974	'Behaviour theory and models of man.' *American Psychologist,* **29,** 859–869.
Barker, R G	1968	*Ecological Psychology: Concepts and Methods for Studying the Environment of Human Behaviour.* Stanford, California: Stanford University Press.
Berntsen, K, & Christiansen, K O	1965	'A resocialization experiment with short-term offenders.' *Scandinavian Studies in Criminology,* **1,** 35–54.
Bion, W R	1961	*Experiences in Groups.* London: Tavistock.
Bottoms, A E, & McClintock, F H	1968	'Research into the institutional treatment of young offenders.' Paper to Third National Conference on Research and Teaching in Criminology, Cambridge University Institute of Criminology.
Bottoms, A E, & McClintock, F H	1973	*Criminals Coming of Age.* London: Heinemann.
Bridgeland, M	1971	*Pioneer Work with Maladjusted Children.* London: Staples Press.
Campbell, J	1965	'Success rates of T S Formidable.' *Approved Schools Gazette,* **59,** 298–9.
Clarke, R V G, & Cornish, D B	1972	*The Controlled Trial in Institutional Research— Paradigm or Pitfall for Penal Evaluators?* London: HMSO.
Clarke, R V G, & Martin, D N	1971	*Absconding from Approved Schools.* London: HMSO.
Cliffe, M J, Gathercole, C, & Epling, W F	1974	'Some implications of the experimental analysis of behaviour for behaviour modification.' *Bulletin of the British Psychological Society,* **27,** 390–397.
Cornish, D B	1973	'Some evaluations of institutional programmes.' *Community Schools Gazette,* **66,** 702–709.
Craft, M	1965	'A follow up study of disturbed juvenile delinquents.' *British Journal of Criminology,* **5,** 55–62.
Craft, M, Stephenson, G, & Granger, C	1964	'A controlled trial of authoritarian and self governing regimes with adolescent psychopaths.' *American Journal of Orthopsychiatry,* **34,** 543–554.
Davies, M, & Sinclair, I	1971	'Families, hostels, and delinquents: an attempt to assess cause and effect.' *British Journal of Criminology,* **11,** 213–229.
Dunlop, A	1975	*The Approved School Experience.* London: HMSO.
Empey, L T, & Lubeck, S G	1971	*The Silverlake Experiment: Testing Delinquency Theory and Community Intervention.* Chicago: Aldine Publishing Co.
Fairweather, G W, Sanders, D H, Maynard, H, & Cressler, D	1969	*Community Life for the Mentally Ill: An Alternative to Institutional Care.* Chicago: Aldine.

Flanagan, J C	1954	'The critical incidents technique.' *Psychological Bulletin*, **51**, 327–358.
Franklin, M E	1966	*Q-Camp: An Experiment in Group Living with Maladjusted and Anti-Social Young Men.* London: Planned Environment Therapy Trust.
Gilbert, D C, & Levinson, D J	1957	'"Custodialism" and "humanism" in mental hospital structure and in staff ideology.' In Greenblatt, M, Levinson, D J, & William, R H (Eds) *The Patient and the Mental Hospital.* Glencoe, Illinois: The Free Press.
Gill, O	1974	*Whitegate: An Approved School in Transition.* Liverpool University Press.
Glueck, S, & Glueck, E T	1934	*One Thousand Delinquents: Their Treatment by Court and Clinic.* (Reprinted 1965). New York: Kraus Reprint Corporation.
Golding, S L	1975	'Flies in the ointment: methodological problems in the analysis of the percentage of variance due to persons and situations.' *Psychological Bulletin*, **82**, 278–288.
Grygier, T	1975	'Measurement of treatment potential: its rationale, method, and some results in Canada.' In, Tizard, J, Sinclair, I, & Clarke, R V G (Eds) *Varieties of Residential Experience.* London: Routledge and Kegan Paul.
Haley, H L	1974	'Social environment therapy: a treatment approach for correctional institutions.' *Canadian Journal of Criminology and Corrections*, **16**, 256–271.
Hammond, W H	1968	'Research into the subsequent histories of a sample of ex-approved school boys.' Paper to a meeting of Approved School Psychologists, Sunningdale.
Harlow, E	1970	'Intensive intervention: an alternative to institutionalization.' *Crime and Delinquency Literature*, **2**, 3–46.
Hartshorne, H, & May, M A	1928	*Studies in Deceit.* Vol. 1. of *Studies in the Nature of Character.* New York: Macmillan.
Healy, W, & Bronner, A F	1928	*Delinquents and Criminals, Their Making and Unmaking: Studies in Two American Cities.* New York: Macmillan.
HMSO	1972	*Statistics relating to Approved Schools, Remand Homes and Attendance Centres in England and Wales for the year 1970.* London: HMSO
Home Office	1969	*The Sentence of the Court.* London: HMSO
Hood, R G	1966	*Homeless Borstal Boys: A Study of their After-Care and After Conduct.* Occasional Papers on Social Administration, No. 18. London: Bell & Sons.
Hunt, G M, & Azrin, N H	1973	'A community-reinforcement approach to alcoholism.' *Behaviour Research and Therapy*, **11**, 91–104.
Jesness, C F	1965	*The Fricot Ranch Study.* California Department of the Youth Authority. (mimeo).
Jesness, C F	1971	'The Preston Typology Study: an experiment with differential treatment in an institution.' *Journal of Research in Crime and Delinquency*, **8**, 38–52.

Jesness, C F, DeRisi, W J, McCormick, P M, & Wedge, R F	1972	*The Youth Centre Research Project.* California: American Justice Institute in co-operation with California Youth Authority. (mimeo).
Jones, H.	1960	*Reluctant Rebels.* London: Tavistock.
Jones, M	1952	*Social Psychiatry.* London: Tavistock.
Kassebaum, G, Ward, D, & Wilner, D	1971	*Prison Treatment and Parole Survival: An Empirical Assessment.* New York: John Wiley.
Kazdin, A E, & Bootzin, R R	1972	'The token economy: an evaluative review.' *Journal of Applied Behaviour Analysis*, **5,** 343–372.
Logan, C H	1972	'Evaluation research in crime and delinquency: a reappraisal.' *Journal of Criminal Law, Criminology and Police Science*, **63,** 378–387.
Martin, D V	1962	*Adventure in Psychiatry: Social Change in a Mental Hospital.* Oxford: Cassirer.
Martinson, R	1974	'What works?—questions and answers about prison reform.' *The Public Interest*, **Spring,** 22–34.
Mathiesen, T	1967	'Resistance to change in correctional institutions.' In, *Collected Studies in Criminological Research, Vol. I.* European Committee on Crime Problems, Council of Europe, Strasbourg.
McKay, H D	1967	'Report on the criminal careers of male delinquents in Chicago.' In, *Task Force Report: Juvenile Delinquency and Youth Crime.* Report on Juvenile Justice and Consultants' Papers. The President's Commission on Law Enforcement and Administration of Justice. Washington: US Government Printing Office.
McKissack, I J	1967	'Are penal methods effective?' *Howard Journal*, **XII,** 131–135.
McMichael, P	1972	*Loaningdale School—A Study of the Impact of an Experimental Regime.* Social Work Services Group, Scotland. (copies obtainable from the author).
McMichael, P	1974	'After-care, family relationships, and reconviction in a Scottish approved school.' *British Journal of Criminology*, **14,** 236–247.
Millham, S, Bullock, R, & Cherrett, P	1975	*After Grace—Teeth; A Comparative Study of the Residential Experience of Boys in Approved Schools.* London: Chaucer Publishing Co Ltd.
Mischel, W	1968	*Personality and Assessment.* New York: Wiley.
Mischel, W	1973a	'On the empirical dilemmas of psychodynamic approaches.' *Journal of Abnormal Psychology*, **82,** 335–344.
Mischel, W	1973b	'Towards a cognitive social learning reconceptualization of personality.' *Psychological Review*, **80,** 252–283.
Moos, R H	1973	'Conceptualizations of human environments.' *American Psychologist*, **28,** 652–665.
Moos, R H	1974	*Evaluating Treatment Environments: a Social Ecological Approach.* New York: Wiley—Interscience.
Morris, A	1971	'A correctional administrator's guide to the evaluation of correctional programs.' *Correctional Research, No. 21.* Boston: Massachusetts Correctional Association.

Mott, J	1973	'Relationship between scores on the Jesness Inventory and reconviction for approved school boys.' *Community Schools Gazette*, **67**, 212–214 and 220–221.
Rapoport, R	1960	*The Community as Doctor*. London: Tavistock.
Rendel, L	1959	*The Caldecott Community: A Survey of Forty-Eight Years*. Ashford, Kent: The Community.
Roberts, K, White, G, & Parker, H	1974	*The Character-Training Industry: Adventure-Training Schemes in Britain*. Newton Abbot: David & Charles.
Robison, J, & Smith, G	1971	'The effectiveness of correctional programs.' *Crime and Delinquency*, **17**, 67–80.
Schwitzgebel, R K	1971	*Development and Legal Regulation of Coercive Behavior Modification Techniques with Offenders*. National Institute of Mental Health, Center for Studies of Crime and Delinquency, Maryland.
Scott, P D	1964	'Approved school success rates.' *British Journal of Criminology*, **4**, 525–556.
Shaw, M	1974	*Social Work in Prison*. London: HMSO.
Sinclair, I A C	1971	*Hostels for Probationers*. London: HMSO.
Sinclair, I A C, & Clarke, R V G	1973	'Acting-out behaviour and its significance for the residential treatment of delinquents.' *Journal of Child Psychology & Psychiatry*, **14**, 283–291.
Sonquist, J A	1970	*Multivariate Model Building: The Validation of a Search Strategy*. Survey Research Centre, Institute for Social Research. Ann Arbour: University of Michigan.
Street, D, Vinter, R D, & Perrow, C	1966	*Organization for Treatment: a Comparative Study of Institutions for Delinquents*. New York: The Free Press.
Stumphauzer, J S	1973	*Behaviour Therapy with Delinquents*. Springfield, Illinois: Charles C Thomas.
Tharp, R. G, & Wetzel, R J	1969	*Behavior Modification in the Natural Environment*. New York: Academic Press.
Tizard, J, Sinclair, I, & Clarke, R V G (Eds)	1975	*Varieties of Residential Experience*. London: Routledge and Kegan Paul.
Warren, M Q	1971	'Classification of offenders as an aid to efficient management and effective treatment.' *Journal of Criminal Law, Criminology and Police Science*, **62**, 239–258.
Weeks, S Ashley	1958	*Youthful Offenders at Highfields*. Ann Arbor: University of Michigan Press.
Wheeler, S, Cottrell, S L (jr), & Romasco, A	1967	'Juvenile Delinquency—its prevention and control.' In, *Task Force Report: Juvenile Delinquency and Youth Crime*. President's Commission on Law Enforcement and Administration of Justice. Report on Juvenile Justice and Consultants' Papers. Washington: US Government Printing Office.
Williams, M	1970	*A Study of Some Aspects of Borstal Allocation*. C P Report No. 33, Office of the Chief Psychologist, Prison Department, Home Office. (mimeo).
Wills, W D	1941	*The Hawkspur Experiment*. London: Allen & Unwin.
Zeitlyn, B B	1967	'The therapeutic community—fact or fantasy?' *British Journal of Psychiatry*, **113**, 1083–1086.

Titles already published for the Home Office

Postage extra

Studies in the causes of Delinquency and the Treatment of Offenders

1. Prediction Methods in Relation to Borstal Training
by Dr Herman Mannheim and Leslie T Wilkins. £1·15
2. Time Spent Awaiting Trial
by Evelyn Gibson. 27p
3. Delinquent Generations
by Leslie T Wilkins. 16p
4. Murder
by Evelyn Gibson and S Klein. 30p

5. Persistent Criminals
by W H Hammond and Edna Chayen. £1·25
6. Some Statistical and other Numerical Techniques for Classifying Individuals
by P. McNaughton-Smith 17½p
7. Probation Research. A Preliminary Report
by S Folkard, K Lyon, M M Carver, and E O'Leary. 42p
8. Trends and Regional Comparisons in Probation (England and Wales)
by Hugh Barr and E O'Leary. 25p
9. Probation Research. A Survey of Group Work in the Probation Service
by H Barr. 40p
10. Types of Delinquency and Home Background. A Validation Study of Hewitt and Jenkins' Hypothesis
by Elizabeth Field. 14p
11. Studies of Female Offenders
by Nancy Goodman and Jean Price. 30p
12. The Use of the Jesness Inventory on a Sample of British Probationers
by Martin Davies. 11p
13. The Jesness Inventory: Application to Approved School Boys
by Joy Mott. 17½p

Home Office Research Studies

1. Workloads in Children's Departments
by Eleanor Grey. 37½p
2. Probationers in their Social Environment
by Martin Davies. 87½p
3. Murder 1957 to 1968.
by Evelyn Gibson and S Klein. 60p
4. Firearms in Crime
by A D Weatherhead and B M Robinson. 30p
5. Financial Penalties and Probation
by Martin Davies. 30p
6. Hostels for Probationers
by Ian Sinclair. £1·15
7. Prediction Methods in Criminology
by Frances H Simon. £1·25
8. Study of the Juvenile Liaison Scheme in West Ham 1961 to 1965
by Marilyn Taylor. 35p
9. Explorations in After-Care
by Ian Sinclair, Martin Silberman, Brenda Chapman and Aryeh Leissner. 85p
10. A Survey of Adoption in Great Britain
by Eleanor Grey. 95p

11. Thirteen-year-old Approved School Boys in 1962
by Elizabeth Field, W H Hammond and J Tizard. 35p

12. Absconding from Approved Schools
by R V G Clarke and D N Martin. 85p

13. An Experiment in Personality Assessment of Young Men Remanded in Custody
by H Sylvia Anthony. 52½p

14. Girl Offenders Aged 17 to 20 years
by Jean Davies and Nancy Goodman. 52½p

15. The Controlled Trial in Institutional Research
by R V G Clarke and D B Cornish. 29p

16. A Survey of Fine Enforcement
by P Softley. 47p

17. An Index of Social Environment
by Martin Davies. 47p

18. Social Enquiry Reports and the Probation Service
by Martin Davies. 36½p

19. Depression, Psychopathic Personality and Attempted Suicide in a Borstal Sample
by H Sylvia Anthony. 36½p

20. The Use of Bail and Custody by London Magistrates' Courts Before and After the Criminal Justice Act 1967
by Frances Simon and Mollie Weatheritt. 57p

21. Social Work in the Environment
by Martin Davies. £1·10

22. Social Work in Prison
by Margaret Shaw. £1·45

23. Delinquency amongst Opiate Users
by Joy Mott and Marilyn Taylor. 41p

24. IMPACT. Intensive matched Probation and After-Care Treatment. Vol. 1. The design of the probation experiment and an interim evaluation
by M S Folkard, A J Fowles, B C McWilliams, W McWilliams, D D Smith, D E Smith and G R Walmsley. 59p

25. The Approved School Experience
by Anne B Dunlop. £1·22

26. Absconding from Open Prisons
by Charlotte Banks, Patricia Mayhew and R J Sapsford. 95p

27. Driving while Disqualified
by Sue Kriefman. £1·22

28. Some Male Offenders' Problems
Part I. Homeless offenders in Liverpool
by W McWilliams.
Part II. Casework with short-time prisoners
by Julie Holborn. £1·80

29. Community Service Orders
by K Pease, P Durkin, I Earnshaw, D Payne and J Thorpe. 75p

30. Field Wing Bail Hostel: The first nine months
by Frances Simon and Sheena Wilson. 85p

31. Homicide in England and Wales 1967–1971
by Evelyn Gibson. 90p

HMSO
Government publications can be purchased from the Government Bookshops at the addresses listed on cover page iv (post orders to PO, Box 569, London, SE1 9NH), or through booksellers.

Prices quoted do not include postage